FROM ROLLERCOASTERS TO CAROUSELS

An Emotional Support Guide to Healing for NICU, Bereaved, and Special Needs Parents

GIGI KHONYONGWA-FERNANDEZ

Published in the United States of America
Printed in the United States of America

Hardcover ISBN: 978-1-0683354-2-6
Paperback ISBN: 978-1-0683354-0-2
eBook 978-1-0683354-1-9

This publication is designed to present information pertaining to the subject matter covered. It is sold with the understanding that the author and publisher are not providing psychological services. The author has neither liability nor responsibility to any individual with regard to any loss or harm caused, or alleged to be caused directly or indirectly, by the material in this book. The fact that an individual, organization, or website is referenced in this work as a citation and/or potential source of further information does not mean that the author or the publisher endorses the information the individual, organization, or website may provide or recommendations that it may make.

Permission:
To obtain permission for reprints and excerpts,
https://familiesblossoming.com
email: gigi@familiesblossoming.com

TABLE OF CONTENTS

DEDICATION, INSPIRATION, and THANKS

Dedication

"As iron sharpens iron, so one person
sharpens another."

—Proverbs 27:17

I would not have had the confidence or bravery to show my vulnerability and put pen to paper to write this book if it were not for my husband and partner-in-life, love, and laughter, Jesús. My iron sharpener. Thank you from the bottom of my heart for everything but particularly for your deep belief in and unwavering support of me, constant reminders that I had something to give to the world, affirmations to "let it flow," cheering me on when I frequently doubted myself, holding down the fort while I disappeared daily into my writing space during this process, ability to make me laugh when I needed it the most, and your sometimes annoying but always accurate critiquing skills. These precious gifts from you have both kept me sane and lifted me up during my first foray into becoming an author. You are the wind beneath my wings, my greatest support, biggest cheerleader, and I love you always.

Inspiration

> "The best and most beautiful things in the world
> cannot be seen or even touched—they must be
> felt with the heart."

> —Helen Keller

To Alejandro, my son, my inspiration, my best and most beautiful thing. I love you more than you'll ever know. Your mere existence is the reason behind this book. What an honor it is for me to have a front row seat to your beautiful life, thirst for joy, brilliant intelligence, infectious laughter, copious amounts of silliness, deep compassion for others, stubbornness when it matters, continuous breaking down of barriers, carving out your own unique path, and defying others' expectations of you. Witnessing all of this fills my heart with joy and makes me want to do better. Be better. As the American children's author and cartoonist, Theodor Seuss Geisel (aka Dr. Seuss), wrote in his book *Happy Birthday to You*:

"Today you are you! That is truer than true! There is no one alive who is you-er than you!"

Keep on being YOU Alejandro, my heart with legs, and keep on inspiring us all.

Thanks

There are way too many people to thank, but here are a few I feel compelled to give a massive shout-out to.

- My family: There is a large group of very special people related to me; bless them, who, although not fully understanding this slightly quirky, free-spirited, wild child of a relative in their midst, have always consistently given me their love and support throughout my life. Space doesn't allow me to name each of them individually as that would take up all the pages of this book, but I must give my heartfelt thanks to four beautiful, very special, and fiercely strong women, namely my mother, Dorothy, and my three sisters, Yvonne, Felicia, and Shunda. Thank you for always cheering on your nutty daughter and sister over the years and for laughing at and with me. Both were needed. Love you loads. A big shout-out is also in order for my many uncles, aunts, cousins, nieces, and nephews who make up my big "ole Southern family" and always shower me with goodness. You know who you are and that you are loved.

- Dr. Edith "Edie" McCarthy for being you: There are not that many physicians who are as present and compassionate as you. You always made a point to see your tiny patients and their parents and families as humans first and patients second. I'm not sure you truly understood what a massive difference that made in our lives and the lives of others. As a highly skilled neonatologist, your keen awareness of the precariousness of the NICU (Neonatal Intensive Care Unit), the vulnerability and strength of the babies and families there, and the long-term physical and emotional implications of being in that space, gives you a unique perspective, which you don't take for granted. This shows your humility, but what stands out the most about you, is your complete respect for the babies and families who inhabit the NICU space and keenness to hear their voices, whether they are silent or loud. You are a clinician with heart and empathy, and it shows. Thank you for agreeing to write the Foreword to this book as well. It means a lot.

- Danielle Perlin-Good: (https://www.thesoulalignedghostwriter.com) - My incredible book coach, editor, and connector. You're simply the best. From the moment we unintentionally met, you believed I was an author-storyteller-thought leader and told me so. I did not have the same belief initially, but this did not stop you from making it your intention to ensure my voice was shared with the world. Finally pouring out onto paper all the words which had been residing in my head and heart for years, was frightening, but my confidence and writing skills increased because of your belief in me. Thank you for your writing knowledge, active listening, cheering me on, sage advice, patience, and gentle challenging for me to think big, during the intense writing process. Your ability to compassionately align with your clients doesn't go unnoticed, and it's fitting that "soul-aligned" is a part of your brand. You always ended our conversations by saying, "I appreciate you", so I am saying the exact thing back to you.

- Rick Lite: (https://stressfreebookmarketing.com/) – My publishing and marketing expert. As your tagline says, you truly are the 'Voice Above the Noise', and boy oh boy was there a lot of loud and conflicting noise – mainly in my head – during this part of the process. Thank you for your calm, succinct, professional, and flexible manner and approach as you guided me through the unfamiliar and sometimes disconcerting spaces of publishing and marketing for my debut book. This combination of attributes kept me focused on the key things at hand but also helped to calm me down when I started to overthink or become anxious about deadlines or the process. Thanks also for not only sharing your expertise and honesty about what made sense and what didn't, but also always giving me the options and ownership to decide which direction I wanted to go. By doing this, my voice was always heard. You were an integral part of getting this book to and across the finish line and out into the world. For that, I'm eternally grateful.

- Parent Contributors: There are no words that are sufficient enough to express my sincere thanks to every single parent around the world who sat down with me to be interviewed and shared their emotional journeys via sharing their hearts, thoughts, and stories. I won't list each of you by name, but you know who you are, and that you are very special to me. I sincerely hope I have honored your experiences and elevated your voices with dignity, and please know that I hold you and your stories close to my heart. I am forever indebted to you for trusting me enough to share pieces of your pain and joy with me and allowing me to share those pieces with the world. Your voices add a special kind of magic to this book and provide even more depth and realness for its readers. They show that although we're a community who has experienced a shared deep trauma, pain, and loss, we're also one that's full of resilience and illuminates hope. You remind us that we are strong and not alone on this journey.

- Professional Contributors: We can often forget that clinicians and professionals have feelings too, which shape their perspective and the way they care for others. Sometimes at the expense of caring for themselves. Thank you to each professional who shared with me your insight, expertise, and personal experiences with babies, families, the healthcare culture and system, the concept of trauma and need for healing. I appreciated your honesty about the challenges of often working within difficult, highly vulnerable, and intense spaces and situations, while trying to promote healing and create meaningful change in people's lives. A continuous balancing act between sadness and hope. Your thoughts were full of wisdom as well as care and consideration for the most vulnerable. I learned so much and value each of you.

- Beta Readers: Priceless jewels you are. Your critique and honest feedback enriched this book beyond measure and made it better. Thank you for being willing to take on this mammoth task with such grace, kindness, gusto, and seriousness. You were the eyes, ears, and hearts of the reader and your voice and perspective mattered. I am grateful beyond measure and thank you from the bottom of my heart.

- Book Reviewers: My amazing cheering squad! If I could bottle up your eagerness and approval, I would do it a thousand times over. My deepest and sincere thanks for taking the time to read my words, provide your honest reviews and opinions, and enthusiastically offer your positive recommendations to encourage others to buy this book. It means a lot.

- NICU, Bereaved, and Special Needs parents around the world: Lastly but surely not least, to every single parent who has experienced or is experiencing the lasting emotional traumatic effects of the NICU, Bereavement, and Special Needs spaces, this book is for you. Regardless of if your experience was 30 years ago or this week, always remember that you are incredible, amazing, resilient, strong, not alone—and most importantly, that healing is possible and real.

FOREWORD

Dr. Edith "Edie" McCarthy
(Neonatologist and Pediatrician)

After serving as a board-certified neonatologist for seven years in the neonatal intensive care units (NICU) of both New York University (NYU) Langone Hospital and Bellevue Medical Centers, located in New York City, I realized that infants who had been born prematurely or with some form of medical fragility needed a higher level of pediatric care after leaving the highly monitored, intensely supportive environment of the NICU. The families of these newborns also needed extra support after leaving the NICU to care for their infant, who may be on special medications, need special equipment for feeding or breathing, or may be at risk for developmental delays or need sub-specialist care. That is why I started Care Intensive Pediatrics, so that I could help the families of preemies to navigate their new reality and help the babies themselves to get off to a great start as NICU graduates.

I met Gigi Khonyongwa-Fernandez in 2008 when she brought her son Alejandro to see me. Alejandro, who was two years old at the time, had been born extremely preterm at 24 weeks gestation. He was born in London, England, and had suffered a complication of his extreme prematurity, which was visual impairment (aka retinopathy of prematurity) likely secondary to oxygen toxicity, which left Alejandro legally blind. Gigi said she had heard about my practice online and was thrilled that my background could help her navigate the best care for Alejandro. Gigi was clearly a great mom, absolutely driven to give her son the best possible life and outcome. This led her to scour the world to find the top medical center and medical team doing cutting edge research for children like Alejandro with his level of visual impairment. On many occasions, she took him to internationally renowned retinal specialists at William Beaumont Hospital / Associated Retinal Consultants (ARC) in Detroit, Michigan (USA), for retinal surgeries, innovative plasma injections, and anything that could help Alejandro. She continues to do so even today. As I came to care for Alejandro as his pediatrician, I grew closer to his mom, Gigi, and tried to be supportive of her as well. She invited me and my family to her home on several occasions, and I grew very fond of Gigi, her husband, Jesús, and, of course, Alejandro, who turned out to be a very talented musician/pianist. Even after Gigi relocated back to London and I moved to New Jersey and closed my practice, we stayed in touch over the years through Facebook and email. I love seeing posts about Alejandro, who is a budding linguist with four languages and counting and aims to study Japanese Studies in the future. So amazing! I keep in touch through social media, with many of my prior patients who, like Alejandro, are all thriving despite their challenges in infancy. When my practice was really doing well with lots of families of preemies, Gigi helped me host several support groups/lectures for parents of preemies to provide an open forum for discussion of issues faced by families, including marital discord, financial pressures, grief, post-partum depression, "NICU PTSD," etc. Gigi is such a naturally loving, caring, and generous human being, so it was no surprise to me that she went on to become a life coach.

In 2009, Gigi and I discussed writing a book together to highlight the stories of the families of preemies because they really were survival stories. She started interviewing some of the mothers in my practice to get their insight and to chronicle their personal stories of the rollercoaster ride they experienced being the parents of NICU babies. Their trials and tribulations, triumphs and disappointments, moments of terror, horror, and prayer for divine intervention displayed the raw humanistic stories that Gigi wanted to narrate in her book, and that she does narrate in this book. She couples this with the purpose of helping other families going through similar experiences, so they know there is hope, they will come out on the other side, and their lives can take on a new normalcy. I was so thrilled when Gigi told me that after many starts and stops over the years, she had finally written the book, with a focus on the emotional journey NICU, Bereaved, and Special Needs parents go through but often don't talk about or receive consistent support for. I was equally thrilled that she asked me to contribute to her book by writing the Foreword. It is my great honor to be involved in this tremendously important undertaking, which is likely to have a lasting impact for years to come on the often-intertwined lives of families of NICU graduates, as well as Bereaved, and Special Needs parents. Kudos Gigi!

PREFACE

My son was born in August 2006 at 24 weeks. He wasn't expected to survive.

He was barely the size of the palm of my hand, weighing a mere 645 grams (1 pound, 4 ounces).

They say one gets pregnant easily, stays pregnant for nine months, goes through labor, delivers the baby, goes home, and lives their happy life of motherhood.

Voila. Simple, right?

I guess it is, until it isn't. As a young adult, if something went a bit haywire, I would flippantly say the phrase, made famous by John Lennon's lyrics to his 1980 song, *Beautiful Boy*, "Life is what happens to you, while you're busy making other plans." Well, this was truly manifested via the birth of our son. Life happened. My plans didn't.

On the day my waters broke, I was 23 weeks + 5 days pregnant and at home on my computer working on the final part of my dissertation for my post-graduate degree from the London School of Economics and Political Science (LSE). I stood up from my laptop, and I thought, "*Hmmm, why am I incontinent?*" In my state of surrealness, that was the only logical explanation for the liquid running down my legs.

My brain quickly re-engaged, and I suddenly realized that the flowing liquid was amniotic fluid, and I was losing a bunch of it—fast. Grabbing my *What to Expect When You're Expecting* book, I quickly flipped through the pages, trying to desperately find some wisdom and reassurance about what in the world was happening to me. There was none. Towards the end of the book, under the "When something goes wrong" section, there was a tiny blurb that briefly mentioned if your waters break early, call your doctor. Throwing the book on the bed, I simultaneously called my doctor and started praying. My heart was beating so loudly that I felt like it'd left my chest and jumped into my head, pounding away from sheer terror. Terrified because I was still in my 2nd trimester. Far too early for this baby. Far too early for me.

I had experienced this terror before in two different but similar scenarios. First scenario: One year prior to our son's extremely early birth, my husband and I were happily and anxiously awaiting the arrival of our first child. My check-ups were going great, and I had no reason to think that they wouldn't continue to. They didn't. A few weeks into my 2nd trimester, my regular ultrasound appointment revealed there was no longer a heartbeat. I was confused because I'd just heard it beating strongly at my previous appointment a couple of weeks prior, so I couldn't quite wrap my head around how things could change so rapidly. This hit me hard emotionally, and I wept for weeks. Second scenario: A year later, after this loss, I was pregnant again. This time with twins. We were ecstatic, and deep down, a small part of me felt like perhaps these two heartbeats were somehow making up for the one we'd lost a year earlier. Logically, I knew this wasn't true and that every pregnancy, every baby is independent of each other, yet my heart needed something to make it feel better, no matter how illogical. Like the year before, everything was going well, until it wasn't. Since they were twins, I was told that I'd have to be monitored more closely, which seemed normal to me and didn't raise any alarms. Hence, I was devastated to be told at my regular check-up during the early part of my 2nd trimester that one of the twins was no longer living. Another heartbeat gone. Confusion and sadness engulfed me again. I couldn't comprehend what was happening nor the doctor's words explaining that I was experiencing a "vanishing twin." What did that mean? Vanished to where? I silently wondered. How could he be gone when I still saw him on the ultrasound, albeit smaller than his sibling and now without a heartbeat? My initial thought was, "Can't they just go find him and bring him back?" Again, an illogical thought, but in my heart, it made perfect sense. My doctor reassured me that since they were fraternal and didn't share amniotic sacs, there was no reason to think the twin who was still living wouldn't continue to. I felt conflicted upon receiving the ultrasound image of two sacs, two babies, one living and one not. Should I focus on the baby I had or the one I didn't? Either way, I felt deep grief and deep guilt.

Fast forward to a few weeks later, and my waters were now breaking. The amniotic fluid of my living twin was being lost at an alarming rate, per the doctor's assessment. My heart was beating even faster, and I didn't know what to do, feel, or think. Given that I'd already experienced both the loss of his sibling a year before as well as the recent loss of his fraternal twin in utero a few weeks earlier, I could not bear the thought of losing him too.

This possible reality wasn't supposed to be on my radar. Neither was delivering a baby at 5½ months.

The day my waters broke, my husband and I had planned to meet up for dinner that evening with some friends who were visiting London from the USA. Instead, my dissertation was put on hold, and our friends saw me in the hospital instead of at the restaurant. My new take on that John Lennon song lyric I mentioned earlier, was now, "Unmade plans can become your life." They became mine.

About an hour after my waters broke, I was in the hospital being rushed to have an ultrasound to determine if I had any amniotic fluid left and if my son was still alive. I did, and he was. The doctors informed me that although I'd lost about half of my fluid, my son would replenish some of this by urinating. Who knew this could even happen? The medical team told me that their goal was to keep my son inside for as long as possible, with their target goal being 27 weeks, when his chances of survival were higher, and the risks of complications, morbidity, and mortality were lower. That was 3½ weeks from where I was at that moment but felt like a lifetime away. They gave me steroid injections in an attempt to rapidly mature his lungs, and we waited, prayed, and cried. He stayed in for three days. On the 3rd day, during a regular monitoring check, they had difficulty hearing his heartbeat, determined that he was in distress and decided he had to be delivered immediately. My breath shallowed and heart raced because I knew that he was way too early to be outside of my womb. I didn't have much time to contemplate this though because within an hour, I'd been prepped and wheeled inside the delivery room for an emergency caesarean section (C-section).

The delivery room was packed with teams of people, including the obstetrics surgical team, Neonatal Intensive Care Unit (NICU) team, and anesthesiology team, all waiting and ready for the birth of our son. My husband and I were waiting there too, of course, but we were not ready. I closed my eyes and tried to breathe as I felt tugs and deep pressure on my stomach. I'm not sure how much time went by, but at some point, I opened my eyes to the surgeon's exclamation that my son was out. I heard the gentle and quiet whisper of the anesthesiologist, who was standing at my head, saying, "He's so tiny."

I also heard something else. Silence. Silence from my son. He didn't cry when he was born, and for several minutes, I didn't know if he was alive or not. Finally, while the surgeons were closing me up on the operating table, I heard somebody in that crowded delivery room call my husband over to see our son. I breathed a sigh of relief because surely, they wouldn't call him over to see a dead baby, would they? I decided that they would not. Our son had made his unexpected and extremely early appearance into this world via an emergency C-section. He'd been in a transverse breech position, which had caused his distress earlier and necessitated the C-section. My life as I knew it had changed, but at that moment, I didn't exactly understand how much.

In the hospital, I learned that I'd experienced Preterm Premature Rupture of the Membranes (PPROM), which is when the amniotic sac ruptures or breaks open before 37 weeks. Although the reasons for my PPROM remain unknown, which admittedly still bothers me, at least I had a name for my gushing loss of amniotic fluid.

An audible gasp left my lips when I finally saw this minuscule human body for the first time in the NICU many hours after he had been born. Sitting in a wheelchair because my legs were still not functioning from the epidural given to me before my C-section, I couldn't quite make out or comprehend what I was seeing.

We had not even thought of a name for our son yet, but there he was, lying in front of me inside an incubator. His translucent skin barely concealed the shapes of his microscopic organs underneath it. Fine silky-like hair was all over his body, and I instantly realized that I was seeing something I wasn't supposed to see. My child was supposed to be tucked away snugly in the warmth and protection of my womb until his skin was no longer translucent, his organs were fully developed and not visible, and his skin was hairless and smooth. Instead, he was splayed out in an incubator like that frog in my high school biology classes decades earlier. His underdeveloped body was on full display for all to see. A rush of regret, guilt, anger, fear, and sadness hit me all at once, and I felt like such a failure. I couldn't keep him safely inside of me away from all this madness. His still developing body wasn't ready to be exposed to the harshness of this world yet, and definitely not the noise, overstimulation, and pain of the NICU. Yet here he was under bright lights, in an incubator, eyes covered, on a ventilator, and with what looked like hundreds of tubes coming out of every single orifice on his tiny body. The small circular holes in his incubator allowed my pinkie finger to touch and completely encircle his wrists, but the incubator itself prevented the natural mother/child touch and connection that only a cuddle could provide. A cuddle I couldn't give him, at least for now. Outside of the womb, he was a touchable untouchable. Born at 24 weeks with a 645 gram birthweight, he was a far cry from the 2.5 kgs to 4 kgs (i.e., 5½–8 pounds) and 40 weeks that constitutes an average size baby and full-term pregnancy.

Taking in my reality, or at least trying to, I simultaneously felt deep shock and intense fear the first time I saw him. Shock that he was here four months before he, my husband, or I were ready and scared of loving him for fear of losing him. Was he even real? Could he even survive? Could anyone survive after being born that early? Could I survive? Physically, mentally, emotionally?

I wasn't so sure. Despite thinking of myself as a proactive, confident person who could handle anything, at this moment, all those adjectives felt foreign to me, and I definitely felt like I couldn't handle much. Fade to black as I suddenly felt nauseous and promptly vomited as the nurse quickly wheeled me out of the NICU and away from my son. I wasn't sure I would ever see him alive again.

The Messy Middle

He was in the NICU one week shy of six months. That's 177 days or 25 weeks of trauma, no matter how you calculate it.

It was a very slow, incredibly abnormal, and stressful experience that masqueraded itself as normal. There were many twists and turns, cheers and tears, super highs, and even deeper lows. I lost count of how many times our son coded, which is the medical term for when your heart and/or breathing stops and you have to be resuscitated. I can't remember the number of life-saving procedures and operations he had. Even after leaving the NICU, surgeries, medical procedures, and specialist check-ups were and still are a regular part of his life many years later, with each one carrying its own share of risks, stresses, and uncertainties. For example, the retinal disease he developed as a consequence of his extreme prematurity, which I'll share more about later, causes glaucoma and hemorrhaging, which he's experienced, and can lead to loss of his eyes, which he hasn't, but the risk remains. Hence, every bi-annual visit to his retinal and glaucoma specialists continues to make me apprehensive, as I hope for the best but a small part of me is still expecting the worst. Nothing could have ever prepared me for any of this. Days, months, and years of varying degrees of uncertainty and unsettledness became my life.

All of this was going on inside my head and my heart. I was on an emotional rollercoaster that I didn't pay to ride and couldn't get off, no matter how hard I tried or loudly I screamed.

During our time in the NICU, and long after we'd left, a whirlwind of strong and sometimes conflicting emotions crept up. Emotions such as fear, anger, guilt, grief, anxiety, sadness, joy, depression, happiness, shock, uncertainty, awe, worry, hope, and overwhelm, to name a few. They hit me in waves either all together or one after the other, almost drowning me at different points along my journey.

NICU Paradox

In the NICU, I observed that the tiny and sick babies there were being 100% supported and cared for every second of their lives, which I totally understood. On the contrary, though, their parents, those big, adult beings who were trying to emotionally balance being on this increasingly rapid emotional rollercoaster, were not. They were left to fend for themselves, and I saw them repeatedly fall off that rollercoaster, several times a day. Sometimes silently and sometimes loudly, sometimes with their individual masks on and sometimes with their raw anguish laid bare and in full view for all to see.

Parents, who were supposed to be the superglue that held everything together for their children, were falling apart. Many of them, including me, became so fixated on our sick children, and understandably so, that we lost ourselves in the process. Equally, the doctors, nurses, midwives, health systems, etc. were also wrapped up in this baby-focused and parent-forgotten dynamic.

This decreased focus on the parents led me to question sometimes whether I was even a mother.

Could I really be called one if my babies didn't come home with me or if I couldn't keep my surviving baby safe in my womb?

I remember reading in my medical notes years after we'd left the NICU that I had been officially classified as "not having successful pregnancies." I learned later that this was my classification because four of my pregnancies had ended in the first and second trimesters, and my surviving baby was born extremely prematurely. I say four because I became pregnant two more times in the years following my son's early birth but lost them as well. In the medical world, my body and I were deemed a failure. Of course, this is not what my notes said, or what any medical professional verbally told me, but is what I understood from reading those words in my medical record, written in black and white, for all to see. Acute feelings of guilt, shame, grief, and inadequacy came rushing back.

In the NICU, there is a continuous battle between life and death happening around you daily. I vividly remember the first time other parents and I were quickly ushered out of the NICU one day. Moments later, I heard the heartbreaking wails of the parents mourning the death of their baby, whose incubator was near my son's. This would not be the only time, and each loss caused me deep sadness and chipped away at any emotional reserve I thought I had. Babies are not supposed to die or fight every second for every breath they take. Parents are not supposed to witness either of these, but this is the NICU paradox. What is not supposed to be is, and what is supposed to be isn't. I soon realized that the people who needed the most emotional support to deal with this seeming never-ending paradox, namely the parents, received the least.

Herein lies the purpose and main reason for me writing this book.

Witnessing this paradox on a regular basis ignited a desire within me to offer parents some sense of normalcy and certainty amid the abnormalities and chaos of the NICU, Bereaved, and Special Needs worlds. To give hope and clarity where there was none. To move forward emotionally, not stay stuck.

The Art of Masking

My initial default coping mechanism for dealing with these feelings was to ignore them and push them way down into the deep crevices of my heart, put on the padlock, and throw away the key. In other words, to mask or hide them. Although reflecting back now, this mechanism seems ludicrous and not the least bit healthy, but at the time it made perfect sense to me. A primary reason for my masking was fear. I was worried and afraid that if the doctors and nurses saw me break down and cry every day, which is what I felt like doing, questions would be raised about whether I could handle motherhood and care for a fragile infant. I imagined Social Services coming to assess me and marking a big, fat "No" next to the question, "Can the mother take care of child?" I have no idea if that question is even on their form, but in my mind, it was, as well as their negative mark.

So, for the five months and three weeks we were in the NICU, it made perfect sense to me to symbolically put on my big girl undies, strap on my super mom cape, wear my "Everything is Good" cap, and show up in the NICU every day with a big smile and positive, confident, and cheerful demeanor. By doing this, I was quickly deemed a "strong parent" by the NICU healthcare professionals and sometimes was even called on to informally support other NICU parents who were thought to be emotionally struggling along their journey. Little did anyone know, I was struggling as well but was too afraid to voice it, believing that my smiling mask hid my struggle and fear.

One reason for donning my trusty mask of positivity and happiness was an attempt to have a reliable shield that was readily available to help me deal with hard emotions such as worry, fear, anger, and frustration without me actually having to deal with them. I falsely believed that my mask would act as a kind of emotional deflector, changing the direction of my emotions away from my heart so they would hurt less. In reality, they hurt more because masks only serve to disguise, not minimize, the pain.

Another reason for my mask-wearing was compartmentalization, which means to keep separate or isolated. According to psychologists, compartmentalization is viewed as a psychological defense mechanism to keep separate any feelings or thoughts we have within ourselves that may appear to conflict with one another. It can be triggered after trauma. Some psychologists feel that a potential advantage of compartmentalization is that it can prevent people from experiencing "cognitive dissonance." This is the mental toll, anxiety, or discomfort a person experiences when their behavior is perceived to be contradictory to their values, beliefs, etc. While I understand that both recognizing you are compartmentalizing and knowing what you are keeping separate may have some benefits, the reality for me was that compartmentalization hindered my progress and healing. For example, I attempted to keep my grief separate from the several losses I'd experienced. Somehow, I thought this separation of the emotion from the event would lessen the blow to my heart by preventing and protecting me from feeling both elements at the same time. I exerted a lot of energy actively trying to keep my emotions away from the lived experience itself. I was not successful.

While my mask had brought calm to those who saw me wear it, it only brought me more confusion. I did not want to feel confused or emotionally lost anymore, and was sick of feeling so alone, despite being surrounded by friends and other NICU parents. My family were supportive, but from afar because I lived and gave birth in a whole different continent and country away from them. It was difficult to express to others how frequently I felt grief, guilt, anger, and disconnection in the same day, hour, or minute. I thought I was going insane, and eventually these feelings were starting to get too heavy and seep out into other areas of my life. My mask was cracking, and pieces of me were falling away with it.

I consistently wore my mask for about another four years after leaving the NICU. I did this by making a point to smile and meticulously, and in hindsight, a bit manically, follow every clinician, therapist, or specialist's instructions for my son to the letter. During those four years, I felt like I was the only parent pretending to have it all figured out. In 2010, we were living in New York City, and while waiting in my doctor's office for an appointment, a magazine stood out among the pile that was stacked on the coffee table. It was simply called Preemie Magazine, and I read each article with rigor because I finally felt like there were other NICU and preemie parents who existed. I wasn't the only one, and this validated my emotions and was an important first step in my healing.

The Rollercoasters

All the NICU, Bereaved, and Special Needs parents I interviewed for this book, as well as countless others I've met along our journey, have described their experience as like being on an emotional rollercoaster. Since the NICU, Bereaved, and Special Needs worlds are often intertwined, this makes the emotional rollercoaster steeper and even more unwieldy and terrifying.

Case in point of these worlds intertwining. I shared earlier about our bereavement through the loss of multiple pregnancies and our experience of being in the NICU. During our long NICU stay, one consequence of our son's survival, was him losing the majority of his sight due to a diagnosis of severe Retinopathy of Prematurity (ROP) that didn't respond to treatment. This is the retinal disease I'd mentioned earlier. His retinas became detached due to the high level of oxygen he needed in order to breathe.

I would later learn that ROP is the same eye disease the American singer, songwriter, and musical genius Stevie Wonder has. In that moment, upon hearing the news that our son was blind, Stevie was the furthest from my mind. As the tears slowly rolled down my cheeks, my first thought was, *He will never be able to see my face.* Just like that, our NICU and bereavement journey was now also a Special Needs one. Another scary, unexpected, and confusing loop had been added to our rollercoaster.

My desire increased to get off or at least slow down this chaotic emotional rollercoaster I was on. Hence, I vowed to myself to not only better understand all the feelings it had induced in me but also to be able to navigate them in a healthier, non-masked way. This prompted my search for a book that highlighted the emotions I felt but rarely spoke about. I wanted reassurance that I was not insane or alone and to know if what I was feeling was normal or not. I wanted to hear from other NICU, Bereaved, and Special Needs parents who understood. I did not want to be left holding onto and being suffocated by my emotions but wanted to know what to do with them. I suppose I was seeking to understand and be understood, a hand to hold, and a light to guide my path. In a nutshell, I wanted to learn how to be in a calmer emotional state, regardless of what curve balls life threw at me.

However, my book search for all the above was not that fruitful. While there were many fantastic, highly valuable books I came across that either detailed individual parents' personal journeys through the NICU, or focused on the medical aspects of prematurity, or looked at the NICU through the professional versus lived experience lens, I didn't come across any that touched on the common emotions parents experienced throughout the trauma trajectory of the NICU, including long after you'd left it. I wanted a book that acknowledged the intersectionality of the many domains of parenting, such as infertility, trauma, prematurity, NICU, bereavement, and special needs that often collide and co-exist. Like me, several parents I interviewed were not solely a NICU parent, solely a Bereaved parent, or solely a Special Needs parent. Often, they've lived or were living at least two of these parenting experiences simultaneously, if not all three. This is why this book intentionally highlights and focuses on them all.

In addition to my own healing, I knew parents who'd also had NICU, Bereavement, and Special Needs experiences and wanted to acknowledge the emotions they felt during them. They also needed reassurance that they were not insane nor alone and guidance and direction on how to manage their emotions in a better way. Parents who also wanted to get off the rollercoaster.

Hence, after our son was discharged from the NICU in February 2007, the seed was planted in my heart to do something about this. Of course, at first, my focus was on our son, making sure I kept him alive at home and being with him during his multiple post-NICU surgeries. Admittedly at times, I didn't feel capable of doing these successfully. Eventually, the seed to help others grew, and the desire to reconcile my emotional head and heart began to take shape via the pages of a book.

Writing the Manual My New World Needed

That seed did not produce any fruit immediately. Although deep down I wanted to do something, I wasn't sure if, when, or how I should go about doing it. I didn't realize how much my parenting experience had traumatized me and knocked my confidence, or how I still needed some type of validation or permission to nourish that seed within.

I did not need to look far.

Around the initial start of my parenting journey, I'd also started exploring a career change. I had been an experienced healthcare clinician and manager for years within health systems in two countries but desired to expand on these skills and expertise and do something different. I still wanted to care for and help people improve their lives, but in a more holistic, compassionate, and forward-moving way. One in which I could partner up with whoever I was working with, to create meaningful, empowering, and, dare I say, joyful solutions for that person's life. I found that in Coaching and retrained to become a Professional Coach.

I realized I could combine my personal experience, and previous clinical and current Professional Coaching expertise to help people address and heal from their rollercoaster of emotional trauma in an authentic and holistic manner. I am bringing all those perspectives into this book, so we work together to move you forward emotionally. My lived parenting experience means I get it. I too have been on the same emotional rollercoaster as you. My professional experiences mean I know how to get you off it. There is a better way, and together, we will find it.

As both a Certified Professional Coach, a Consultant as well as a Trauma-Informed Certified Coach (TICC), my passion is all about helping individuals, teams, and organizations find their joy again. Being a TICC simply means that I have a unique set of skills that helps me to recognize people who have been or still are involved with traumatic events that are preventing them from moving forward in a positive manner. I do this by working in partnership with them to build their confidence and explore how they can move closer to a place of wellness and joy and where they want and need to be. Through coaching my clients over the years and interviewing parents for this book, what I've found to be true is that people want to stop existing in an emotional fog and start living with emotional clarity. They want tangible, effective, and compassionate ways to do this and to feel a sense of community along the way.

I help them achieve this and can help you, too.

Prior to becoming a Professional Coach, I was an experienced healthcare clinician as mentioned before. Specifically, I was a registered Occupational Therapist specializing in neurology and spent almost 20 years working in a range of clinical settings, both as a clinician and manager in the United States (USA) and United Kingdom (UK). Given my specialty, I treated individuals who had an injury or illness to the brain or spinal cord, and through their experiences, saw firsthand how a person's life can change in an instant. A car accident, head injury, brain tumor, spinal cord injury, stroke, or neurodegenerative disease, etc. abruptly changed the lives of the people I was privileged to treat. Although not a medical doctor, these poignant clinical experiences taught me the importance of treating people holistically as an integral part of their recovery. What they experienced emotionally impacted their physical healing and vice versa, and I carried this lesson with me as a senior healthcare manager years later and am continuing to carry it into this book as well. I strongly believe that you can't treat the physical aspects of a NICU, Bereaved or Special Needs experience without addressing the emotional part as well. We'll aim to do this together throughout these pages.

In addition to my personal and professional lens, I also wanted to hear other parent voices to gain insight into their respective emotional journeys to discover if it was just me who had been, and, to be honest, still is at times, emotionally wobbly. I was interested in exploring whether my desire to focus on parents' emotional journeys and their healing from them was even important and worth putting out into the world. Hence, for over a year, I reached out to and interviewed other parents who had lived NICU, Bereavement, and Special Needs experiences, either singularly or combined.

I also reached out to neonatologists, maternal-infant and trauma specialists to gain the clinical and professional perspectives of these emotionally traumatic experiences. In the end, I interviewed:

Almost 50 parents and professionals from across 14 countries and 6 continents

It was a rich mixture of different people, situations, cultures, languages, health systems, resources, and outcomes, but all with very similar emotional journeys. This random global sampling of honest parent and professional voices confirmed to me that the wobbly and frightening emotional rollercoaster that parents, and even sometimes professionals, are on is real, and highlighted this key point:

> ***The seven emotions highlighted in this book are <u>universal</u> and the <u>most common</u> experienced across the globe by NICU, Bereaved, and Special Needs parents…. and really anyone who has experienced trauma.***

You are not alone.

Throughout the pages of this book, you will hear their voices, perspectives, and wisdom. My hope is that you will also feel their support and compassion. As mentioned previously, you will also hear my voice as a fellow NICU, Bereaved, and Special Needs parent coupled with my knowledge as a Professional Coach as we explore strategies for you to move forward. We're in this together, and I will walk alongside you as we work to move you closer towards your own healing.

In my coaching practice, I start wherever my clients are, with the belief that they are whole and capable of getting from point A to point B. They are just blocked by something—sometimes their situation but usually themselves. My job is to walk with them to facilitate their recognizing, uncovering, and tearing down those blocks and turning them into stepping-stones or even throwing them away if they so choose. We do this by being intentionally curious, increasing awareness (what I like to call your "aha" moments), and taking meaningful action. You and I will follow a similar path together in this book. As part of your awareness-building and forward-moving direction of travel, we will explore the two concepts of compartmentalization and processing and how they can hinder or help your healing.

We will also explore trauma. From coaching hundreds of people over the years, I've learned that trauma and its impact on people's lives can manifest itself repeatedly. A recent study showed that, in some cases, the traumatic impact may continue to show up five, ten, or even thirty-plus years later. We will tackle this by exploring trauma a bit more thoroughly, especially against the backdrop of your lived parental experiences and emotional journey.

Intentional Emotions-Focused

Each emotion will be discussed in the format of sections versus chapters. No chapter 1, chapter 2 business. This is intentional because when you pick up this book, I want you to hone in on the emotion that is resonating with you at any given time versus following a first, second, third format. Our emotions and how we experience them are not linear, step-by-step, or chapter-by-chapter, so the way we explore and heal from there should not be either.

My aim as we walk through these pages together is to flip the narrative of trauma for you. This flipping is to help you move further away from feeling lost and closer towards finding yourself again, one emotion at a time. This finding process does and will take time, as the story below shows, so I ask you to be kind to yourself as we walk together.

A German NICU and Bereaved mother of 25-week twins, in which one lived and the other one didn't, shared how it took her 20 years before she did not cry on her surviving child's birthday. She said,

"You look at your child and always think there should be another one."

In her case, multiple layers of grief needed to be processed, and did not happen overnight, but rather over years. You will hear more voices like hers as we walk through this book together. Don't be surprised if some of the voices sound like your own. While the stories and specifics may differ, the emotional journeys that NICU, Bereaved, and Special Needs parents collectively experience are remarkably similar. This again shows the universality of our emotions when experiencing trauma. I hope through this book you realize that you are not alone, and this realization gives you comfort and strength.

I also hope that it gives you resilience or shall I say, remind you of the resilience that you have within regardless of the traumatic experience you have gone or are going through. In reflecting on these experiences, the director of the national prematurity organization in Brazil shared this observation,

"I think it's the most extreme experience that a parent can endure. Not knowing if your baby will survive or what the consequences of a preterm birth could be, but at the same time what has also amazed me has been the strength and resilience of the babies and their parents and the power of life. The most inspiring thing was to witness the ability of preemie parents to see their children's potential, rather than their limitations."

She also mentioned that parents were like *"warriors"*. You may not think of yourself as a warrior, but the definition of a warrior is a person who shows bravery, courage, and vigor in warfare or a fight. Being a NICU, Bereaved, or Special Needs parents is a type of physical and emotional fight, that you didn't intend to do battle in. Yet you have and you are, so perhaps thinking of yourself as a parent warrior just might be something to consider.

As mentioned previously, this book is not designed to be experienced in a linear fashion, but in a where-you-are-at-the-moment manner, meaning you are free and strongly encouraged to explore these pages in the best way that suits you. Ideally, you can pick it up, jump to the section of whatever emotion you're feeling, struggling with, or simply thinking about, delve a bit deeper from an awareness and processing standpoint, fold the pages back, write in it, be cheered on and/or comforted by your like-minded and similar-experienced "tribe" of parents, and work through the actions at your own pace.

Take your time as you do so. This is not a race or mad dash to the finish line. Neither is your healing. Under the Action part of each section, there is a journaling space at the end of each emotion, designed to encourage you to reflect and contemplate on what is coming up for you as you explore that particular emotion, or just simply be.

Lastly, remember that there is no right or wrong way to go through this book or to feel a certain way as you do so. View it as a time to reclaim, find, or even redefine your voice, confidence, and power as a parent while you become more emotionally whole. You've got this, so let's jump in, get started, and do this together.

Where We Are Going Together?

Towards healing and joy.

That is our planned destination and direction of travel. I typically tell my coaching clients that we only look back if it helps us move forward, and I'm telling you the same thing. We won't stay in your emotions just for the sake of staying there, but rather as a means for you to take that next step forward towards healing. I like to call any movement forward the "so what" phase, meaning that once you highlight an issue, what are you going to do about it? For example, once you figure out the emotion that is tripping you up or keeping you stuck-in-a-rut and/or on an emotional rollercoaster, so what? What are you going to do about it? Do you *want* to do anything about it? You can decide to keep it as a stumbling block in your life or take steps to make it a stepping-stone towards your healing and finding of hope. Your healing journey is up to you, but I'm here in your corner, cheering you on and backing you up 100%.

If you've picked up this book, you either have lived experiences as a NICU, Bereaved, and Special Needs parent and their subsequent common emotions, or you have lived through some other form of trauma. Regardless, you know this emotional rollercoaster ride firsthand and the devastating effects it can have on your life if not addressed. I assume you are here because you not only want to address these emotions but also learn how to navigate them in a healthier way. You may also be here just simply to gain a bit of reassurance that you are ok. Or perhaps you are here to know that you are not alone. Whatever the reason you have come, you are in the right place.

How We Will Get There

Via the Carousel. Huh? You may be asking

The aim and trajectory of this book is to give you back some control and get you off your emotional rollercoaster ride and onto one which I propose is a better one. The Carousel.

You may wonder why I chose this ride as a symbol of our destination. I did so because although the carousel is a ride that still moves, it does so at a slower, calmer, and more controlled pace. It feels less scary, and if there is an unexpected dip, it is not as deep, jarring, or wild, so you are more able to manage it. My hope is that you do so in a more intentional, healthier, and joyful way. I will show you how.

My coaching approach and the approach used throughout the pages of this book are transformative in nature. This means that I'm starting with the strong belief that you are not irretrievably broken but rather are whole and highly capable of change, repair, and becoming who you want to be. You just need a bit of help, space, and time to do so. I suppose I have always believed this about people, but trauma has a way of telling you otherwise.

In thinking about my coaching method, it always involves curious inquiry and reflection (what's happening), exploration (why and how it's happening), and actions (how to change what's happening). I listen to what is said but more often and sometimes more importantly to what is not being said and use this to increase awareness, provide acknowledgement, gently challenge, and move forward. This process led to my creation of the Reflection, Exploration, and Action (R.E.A.) model, which is the same approach and methodology I will use in this book.

As I shared earlier, my desire to create this book came from my search to find a book I never had. One that not only understood and spoke the language of my emotions and trauma but more importantly provided a sense of lightness, optimism, guidance, and direction against the often heavy and dark worlds of NICU, Bereavement, and Special Needs parenting. I wanted a book that did not leave me in the NICU (been there, done that), nor left me emotionally wandering at large through the forests of loss and special needs. I wanted a book that was equally serious, funny, honest, practical, and interactive. One I could come back to time and time again at different stages of my emotional journey for clarity and support. A book that "got me," didn't make me feel alone, helped me move forward, and gave me hope.

I am pouring all those desires, coupled with my and others' perspectives and expertise, into this book for you, and my wish is that it gives everything I have just mentioned and then some. Meaning that each time you peruse these pages, you come away emotionally stronger, healthier, and happier.

Six things to remember:

1. This is not a traditional tell-your-story book. Rather, its focus is on the emotional journey that parents are on, but since the emotions are woven within the stories, some elements of the latter will naturally be shared.

2. All emotions parents have experienced won't be discussed. It is impossible to name every single emotion that hits us along this rollercoaster journey, given that some are unique to each parent. The point is to highlight and explore the seven most common ones parents experience.

3. At the risk of sounding like a broken record, again, just like our emotions aren't linear, with one occurring first, then another second, and yet another one third, neither is this book. It's not meant to be read in a linear, chapter-by-chapter format. Rather, it's been intentionally designed for you to pick it up and jump to whatever emotion you're dealing with or want to know more about. Once you are there, ponder its content, jot your thoughts down, connect with other parents' experiences, or practice some of the strategies. Feel free to fold back its pages, put it down, and pick it back up a few days later, either re-starting wherever you left off or jumping to a completely different emotion. This is why there are no chapters, only emotions sections. To help you easily locate each one, I've listed the emotions alphabetically.

4. It is in a workbook style format, inclusive of a mixture of parents' stories, reflective questions, journaling space, coaching tips, and, as my husband often says, "dashes of my 'Gigi-ness." Whether the latter dashes are helpful or not, I am not so sure, but I hope this format gives you the feeling of me walking beside you as you find yourself again and regain your calmness, joy, clarity, and direction.

5. Although the target audience is the NICU, Bereaved, and Special Needs parent populations, it cannot be forgotten that many NICU professionals also experience similar emotions because they are within the same trauma-inducing space that you are. Hence, their voices will also be shared at relevant points throughout these pages.

6. Equally, since trauma can be and often has been experienced by anyone, the content in this book can be beneficial to anyone who feels drawn to its message of healing from trauma.

In addition, this book is not about your child or children, which may sound harsh but is not intended to be. This book is about you, the emotional journey you've experienced or are experiencing, and your continuous healing. It is written with the following seven goals in mind:

1. Explore the most common emotions NICU, Bereaved, and Special Needs parents experience.

2. Allow you time to reflect on your emotional journey.

3. Facilitate you getting off or slowing down your emotional rollercoaster to more of a manageable carousel pace. Of course, even with this, there will still be ups and downs, but my hope is that the speed won't be so fast, the loops not as jarring or extreme, nor the hills too high.

4. Provide you with a road map for healing and emotional wellness through coaching-based and trauma-informed actions, strategies, guidance, and tools you can implement in your life.

5. Walk with you, alongside a compassionate community, who "gets you" and have had similar experiences. We'll do this through the sprinkling of snippets of other parents' voices and stories, including mine, to remind you that you're not alone.

6. Shower you with support. All the parents I interviewed were asked to share any words of wisdom or advice they had for you. They obliged in bucketloads, and you can find their heartfelt, encouraging and supportive words in Appendix 1.

7. Leave you with resources. Many of the parents and professionals I interviewed are experts, pioneers, and change-makers, in their own right. Hence, they have shared a wealth of information that may be beneficial to your understanding and healing. You will find this in the resources section in Appendix 2, listed by continent and country.

As previously mentioned, my created methodology for my coaching approach and what I will use in this book is Reflection, Exploration, and Action (R.E.A.):

1. **Reflection**: Highlighting the myriad of ways to pause and consider where you are emotionally to increase your awareness.

2. **Exploration**: Incorporating space and time for you to contemplate what the emotion means for you and how you either compartmentalize or process it.

3. **Action**: Getting you to think about the next steps of how you can better manage your emotions in a healthier way, via coaching-based strategies and tips.

Journaling:

An integral part of your action will involve journaling, which is writing down your honest personal thoughts, feelings, and experiences so you can better express and process them. I like to say, journaling without self-judgment. By this, I mean to not over-analyze your thoughts but rather get them out of your head where they are ruminating around and out in the open on paper where you can view and explore them more constructively.

Journaling can be done in a structured (i.e., specific template used) or unstructured (i.e., no template, just write) format. I tend to encourage my coaching clients to use the latter format coupled with gentle guidance. In my experience, this promotes freer and more unfiltered thought, which I've found to be the most raw, authentic, and honest. You're more likely to say what you really feel when there are less boundaries.

There are seven (7) common emotions highlighted in this book. At the end of each emotion section, I will ask you to grab a notebook or piece of paper and:

a. Answer three guided questions about that specific emotion, and

b. Write down anything else that is coming up for you about that emotion.

In journaling, there are no right or wrong answers. It's simply a moment for you to pause and be honest with yourself about that emotion and figure out what you need or want from it and what you don't. As you do so, I encourage you to lean into the emotion, without judgement, so you can move forward. For additional guided questions and resources about journaling, feel free to go to my website: www.familiesblossoming.com.

This book is about you unapologetically creating a change within yourself. One that's healing, full of clarity, and designed to move you from where you are now to where you want to be. A change that is unique to you and makes sense for your life. I will be right beside you the entire time.

If you are ready, your journey from emotional trauma to emotional healing starts now.

EMOTION

Emotion: A strong feeling derived from your situation, mood, or relationships.

"He's not going to make it anyway," said the doctor as she quickly switched off the monitors and left the room. The same monitors attached to my stomach, which assured me that our son was still alive in my womb, albeit without that much amniotic fluid to float in mind you, but he was there. Now with that quick flip of a switch and flippant comment, was he? I did not know. I was only a little over 23 weeks pregnant, approximately five ½ months, and had just been admitted to the hospital after my waters broke prematurely. This was not my first pregnancy, but none of my previous pregnancies ended with living children. Hence, I was terrified the one inside of me would suffer the same fate.

My husband and I stared at the closed door with confusion and disbelief. Silence scoured the room as shock made its horrific presence. Did that just happen, or were we imagining it? A few seconds, which felt like several hours, passed by before we jumped into action. My husband rushed out the door, frantically telling anyone who would listen what had just happened. Another doctor quickly came in and swiftly turned all the monitors back on. I had not realized that I hadn't dared to breathe in those moments of uncertainty until I saw those numbers light up and my son's heartbeat (and my breath) reappear. We had never seen that first doctor before and, thankfully, never saw her again.

In an instant, I strongly felt the emotions of both shock and disbelief in equal measures. I don't think that doctor ever realized, or even cared about, the weight and devastation of the emotional bomb she'd dropped on us that day, the implications of it, or the splattering of emotions that would soon follow and continue to this day.

Emotions

Such a loaded word with endless definitions and connotations. The sheer strength of the feelings discussed in this book is a common thread for parents, which can make the emotions appear even more powerful and you, powerless.

Brad Hardie, a Certified Trauma Professional, Master Certified Coach, and Co-Founder of Moving the Human Spirt, a Canadian-based leader in Trauma-Informed Coaching, describes emotions in colors. He shares:

*"When we think about emotions or even when people don't have language to express their emotions, sometimes I ask, 'Well, can you put a color to it?' So, if I think about the emotions or colors that come up the most, especially during fight or flight, one of the colors is red. Emotion is certainly a sense or energy that we may or may not incorporate **into anger or frustration**. Another one is if we think about the feelings of not being able to dislodge or release the energy coming up inside of us, for example, when we're in a place where we can't fight or flight, the emotions move from anger and frustration to complete **disassociation** and show up as **sadness or disconnect**. We might think of this as being blue as a color. These emotions play a huge piece in trauma."*

To say there is a plethora of emotions parents experience when they inhabit the NICU, Bereaved, and Special Needs spaces is an understatement. Some emotions are felt singularly, some alternatively, and some simultaneously, like they are juxtaposed together as a cruel joke. I was joyful that I had just had my baby who was alive, but sad because I couldn't hold him. However your emotions are felt, the point is they exist. Highlighting their existence is one of the purposes of this book.

As mentioned in the preface, I have chosen to intentionally focus on the emotional experiences of NICU, Bereaved, and Special Needs parents. Although their parenting journeys may appear to be separate entities, more times than not, there are both physical and emotional linkages across all three parenting experiences. They are frequently interwoven and sometimes connected to the infertility world as well. A study published in *Sage Journal* noted, "Death is no stranger to the neonatal intensive care unit." Several of the NICU parents I interviewed shared that they'd also experienced loss as well as having a child with special needs.

An Irish NICU mother of a 25-week preterm infant shared the following about the NICU:

"The NICU can sometimes be the end of an incredibly long journey, which has been very circuitous and may have been to the graveyard a few times, the operating theater a few times, and to the fertility clinic a few times."

Imagine trying to come to grips with three life-altering situations: being in the NICU, losing a child, and having a child with special needs. These overlapping emotional wounds and worlds may directly and indirectly have an adverse impact on a person's emotional health.

Another situation that produces big emotions for parents is having a full-term NICU baby, in which parents must deal with the disbelief of others in addition to their own emotions. While all or most babies born prematurely require a NICU stay, not all babies in the NICU are premature. Statistics show that one in ten babies are born prematurely, which is defined as being born 37 weeks or less gestational age, but about 50–60 percent of babies in the NICU are considered full-term (i.e., born at 37+ weeks gestation). During my parent interviews, about 7% were NICU parents of full-term but sick babies, not preemie parents. They all expressed having similar experiences of others making them feel like they didn't belong in the NICU space.

One American NICU mother of a 41-week full-term baby shared that she frequently felt judgment and isolation when someone found out they were in the NICU and asked how early her child was. Upon finding out she was full-term, they would say,

"Full-term babies are not in the NICU," to which she would reply, "Yes, they absolutely are, nearly half of NICU babies are full-term."

She shared that she would sometimes explain: *All preemies are NICU babies, but not all NICU babies are preemies,* which is an important distinction to remember when speaking with NICU parents.

In some countries, the distinction between preterm and full-term babies in the NICU is made even starker by the practice of keeping them separated.

A NICU father of a 29-weeker from Uganda shared that in their hospitals,

"preterm babies and full-term babies are kept in a different section of the hospital, and they don't mix."

I can only imagine that this could cause parents to feel even more isolated within their NICU experience.

Although there are many varied reasons for parents' entry into this surreal world called the NICU, the range of emotions associated with being in that abnormal space are similar. None of the emotions are supposed to be felt in the parenting world that we'd envisioned for ourselves, which was a "normal" parenting experience. I use that word "normal" very loosely because the spectrum of normal can be so vast. In this context, normal can be generally described as "things that happen which are typical, usual, or expected." Nothing about the NICU, Bereavement, or Special Needs parenting experiences is typical, usual, or expected. In the normal scheme of things, babies are not supposed to be in the NICU, not supposed to die, or face a lifetime of additional needs. None of it is supposed to happen, but it does. We, as the parents living in these abnormal, not-supposed-to-happen experiences, must learn to deal with them and all the emotions that come along with them, which sometimes can feel impossible.

Emotions such as those that come with not being able to hold your baby as they lay on the other side of a glass incubator, or never taking your child home, or realizing that the severity of your child's special needs means you may be their caretaker for life, are akin to a heavy weight being attached to you that you aren't sure you can carry. Acknowledging the existence of these emotions does not mean that we love our children any less—nope, not by a long shot. It just means that we frequently have one, two, three, or sometimes four-plus extra layers of parenting issues, challenges, and emotions as part of our parenting journey that we must consider and manage. Extra things that don't even cross the mind of a parent of a "normal" child. For example, when my son came home from the NICU, we were given instructions for him to not be around a lot of people because his lungs were still very compromised, putting him at a higher risk of catching respiratory illnesses such a Respiratory Syncytial Virus (RSV). In children born normal and healthy, this virus can cause the common cold, but in children born prematurely and sick, it can be potentially fatal. I've lost count of how many of our "normal parent" friends did not understand how important our "no visitors" rule was and thought we were being overly protective, and slightly rude, parents.

I wanted to shout out something like this to them: 'a cold to you, a casket for me'.

I realize that may sound a bit dramatic, but during those initial three to five months after he was discharged, I was super vigilant and honestly didn't care about being considered a drama queen. What I want parents and people in general who haven't experienced the NICU, Bereavement, or Special Needs worlds to understand or at least appreciate is this: Parenting looks and feels different to us ... because it is different.

Sometimes I feel that our emotions as parents within the NICU, Bereaved, and Special Needs spaces are not discussed, acknowledged, appreciated, or understood as thoroughly as they should be. This can lead to parents bottling up their emotions, which is not healing or positive, and can leave them believing that the feelings they are experiencing are somehow bad, unusual, irrelevant, or unimportant and should not be shared or expressed. Some examples from the parents I interviewed include:

A British NICU mother of a 26-weeker who shared:

"I was crying as I sat by the incubator of my son but was told by the nurse to leave because my crying wasn't helping my child."

An American mother who experienced the loss of one of her 27-week preterm twins over 40 years ago explained it in this way,

"I didn't have a problem talking about my son's death to others but found that many people were uncomfortable talking about it, so I'd circumvent the conversation to other topics."

A father from the USA of a special needs child shared how he feels some:

"frustration and anger when others throw blanket statements at me, such as 'God gives special kids to special parents."

These types of situations and comments can make parents feel misunderstood and even more isolated in an already isolating experience.

COMMON EMOTIONS

There are a range of different emotions that are felt in varying degrees within the NICU, Bereavement, and Special Needs journeys. During our time together in this book, we will focus on the seven most common ones experienced based on my research and in interviewing almost forty parents across the globe. These are the Emotion sections of this book. Remember, there is no linear step-by-step order of how people experience these emotions, but for ease of reference, I have put them in alphabetical order.

- Anger
- Anxiety
- Fear
- Grief
- Guilt
- Overwhelm/Stress (interconnected)
- Shock/Disbelief (interconnected)

Rarely are these emotions experienced as a stand-alone event, but oftentimes they can overlap, as well as be felt in parallel with each other. Herein lies their power and complexity. The latter two emotions listed were often frequently discussed, experienced, and thought about in pairs, hence the reason they are combined. Any one of these emotions by themselves can knock the wind out of your sails, but when you are experiencing them all at once or back-to-back, several times throughout your life's journey, then you can begin to see why you may feel a bit wobbly on your feet as you try to navigate life.

Within the NICU, Bereavement, and Special Needs spaces, these emotions tend to be long-term and can start manifesting themselves in different situations. For example, you may continue to feel grief for years, causing you to have the need to celebrate and remember your child or children you lost on their day of birth or death. Or you may feel scared or anxious when your former preemie, now teenage child, gets sick because it emotionally takes you right back to the NICU.

Several of these emotions can produce what I will call "emotional by-products," which I define as those unintentional situations experienced that may not be considered an emotion but are a direct result or significant part or outcome of the emotional journey. Take, for instance, relationships with others. Several parents I interviewed shared how their relationships with a wide range of people, including their partner, family, friends, care providers, work colleagues were adversely impacted because of them being a NICU, Bereaved, or Special Needs parent.

One Spanish NICU father described how the isolation he felt from friends was like experiencing what he called,

"Social bankruptcy because we were on our own."

He shared with me further that one of the main reasons he felt this way was because, while his child was in the NICU, he had friends who either left the friendship by not reaching out or friends who did not or could not provide the kind of friendship or emotional and physical support that he needed the most at that time.

Or

A British NICU and Special Needs mother who shared,

"My closest friend from home didn't contact me the whole time my son was in the hospital, and it upset me. Later, she said that she didn't contact me because she didn't know what to say. I was thinking, 'You don't have to know what to say; just say, "I don't know what to say."

Our friendship hasn't been the same since. It's interesting when friends don't acknowledge what has happened to you and are silent—what that does to the friendship.

In each of these cases, the friendships deteriorated. Hence, an emotional by-product of overwhelm and stress of the situation could be Relationship Tension/Breakdown. This by-product doesn't just show up in friendships as shared above, but also within marriages and partnerships as well. Although there is not enough hard data to say that the NICU, Bereavement, or Special Needs experiences increase the risk of marital breakdown as it hasn't been studied enough, there has been some literature suggesting that the death of a child could have detrimental effects on the marriage relationship, and parents of seriously or chronically ill children can be at a higher risk of divorce.

One NICU and Special Needs mother from the USA shared her experience with this by-product in the following way.

"While we were in the NICU, we had to put everything on the back burner, including our relationship."

This led to their marriage breaking down, in part, because of their NICU stay.

These by-products show the expansiveness, complexity, and impact of the emotions parents face. Hence, it is important that they are acknowledged and incorporated into the healing process, as/if appropriate.

As we walk through the seven emotions throughout the pages of this book, I invite you to consider viewing each of them from both a collective and individual perspective. Reflect on how an emotion has affected you overall or within a specific area of your life. Feel free to think of your emotions as colors if you so wish, as Brad Hardie described them earlier. However, you decide to view them, again, be sure to give yourself grace and space, and refrain from any self-judgment. I'm intentionally repeating this because I know how easy and unhelpful it is for us to be self-critical even over things we have no control over.

If you find yourself grappling with anger or that you haven't quite fully processed your guilt, or you're feeling overly anxious about anything related to your child, 5, 10, or 20+ years since you started on your parenting journey, know that this is completely okay.

Trauma

A deeply distressing, disturbing, stressful, and frightening event that is difficult to cope or deal with.

We cannot properly explore and delve into the common emotions without discussing the elephant in the room called trauma. Although trauma is not an emotion per se, nor is this a trauma book, it was such a prominent part of parents' vocabulary, their emotional journeys and experiences that I felt it is an essential topic to highlight. I do not profess to be the expert on this topic, but based on both empirical and research data, trauma is the permanent backdrop throughout the NICU, Bereavement, and Special Needs spaces. Studies show that parents who have a baby receiving care in the NICU will likely experience emotional distress and are at an elevated risk of experiencing trauma, especially with the substantial risk of neonatal death.

You will see this permeate throughout the pages of this book because we cannot speak about the most common emotions without speaking about trauma and vice versa. As a Trauma-Informed Certified Coach, I see trauma manifest itself in my clients' personal and professional lives. We work together to dislodge it from dominating their lives so they can move forward.

What I hope we will achieve in highlighting trauma now is that by viewing and understanding your emotions through the trauma lens, you will be better informed and equipped to heal from or at least mitigate trauma's impact on your life.

Trauma forever alters the human psyche, heart, and perspective.

It changes the way we speak, think, and show up in the world. You cannot go back to a pre-trauma you, but you can use that traumatic experience to inform your next steps, to help you navigate people, situations, and your heart in a way that soothes your soul and shines light on your path. This is my hope for you as we walk through this space together. Brad Hardie explains it this way:

"We need two things: a) An awareness that this condition of trauma can pass, and b) that you can't heal alone. These two things are difficult to do, but I can say 'pass' on any trauma I'm experiencing. Because we make choices every day about whether we will pass or not, how we're going to engage within our environment, whether we're going to share our emotions, who we're going to share them with and who we're not going to share them with."

Trauma can be characterized into three types:

- **Acute**: a single event such as an accident

- **Chronic**: repeated and prolonged as in domestic abuse, or

- **Complex**: exposure to varied and multiple traumatic events, such as war and famine

In his book *Trauma, The Invisible Epidemic*, physician and psychiatrist Dr. Paul Conti talks about another type of trauma, which is:

- **Vicarious:** Feeling the emotions of others to the point of internalizing their suffering, such as doctors and nurses feeling your pain. It has also been described as the emotional residue due to the exposure of traumatic stories and experiences of others.

Let us pause for a moment here because this type of trauma is one that we can be less aware of, but it is important to know how it might show up in your emotional journey. One way is through your care professional or provider. By professional, I mean doctors, nurses, other health care providers, social workers, teachers, psychologists, etc. They can and do experience trauma. They have hearts like us and some of them are not afraid to show it. Some examples of vicarious trauma witnessed by parents include:

An American NICU mother of a 29-weeker described how when she was being induced in the delivery room, the anesthesiologist standing at her head:

"started crying, and I felt her tears hitting my forehead."

Another NICU and bereaved mother from the USA of 25-week preterm triplets described this vivid memory of both her neonatologist and parent liaison:

"When we brought [my daughter] to the emergency room, I had her in a stroller, and [after she unexpectedly died there], I just remember them walking out of the hospital together with us pushing that stroller that was now empty."

As I write this, I am acutely aware that this is not the case with every clinician or professional you have met along your journey. Some have not exhibited compassionate, professional, or even knowledgeable care, which probably left you wondering why they were even in a field that serves humanity. Unfortunately, I've come across countless ones who fall within this category, and during my parent interviews, several also shared incidents in which they felt provider compassion was frequently missing. Thankfully, my path has also been full of professionals who got it and were and are intuitively aware and respectful of the fact they were in a delicate space of human vulnerability with parents and families and showed up accordingly.

One NICU therapist from the USA shared that:

"the NICU space around the baby and family was a sacred, privileged space I'm entering into. I felt like I was and needed to be considered the visitor in their lives, instead of the families being considered the visitors in their own babies' space"

In considering vicarious trauma from the professional's perspective, during my interviewing of approximately ten professionals globally for this book, vicarious trauma existed for the majority of them. Several stated that when their patients experienced trauma, they did as well.

One neonatologist from the USA shared,

"I cannot forget the very sad times where I had to tell parents that we did everything we could, and I was going to have them hold their baby to say goodbye. That they could take as long as they needed. I just remember feeling helpless."

Another American neonatologist shared,

"I could see and feel the fear and sadness, knowing what parents were going through, and really wanted to say to parents that we were struggling on this side of it too."

The challenge for professionals is that they often do not have a safe place to express the emotional trauma they experience. This can lead them to push down their emotions and put on their "professional" mask, which may adversely impact their interaction and engagement with you. Not because they don't want to engage, but in an effort to minimize their own trauma, they may not be able to fully engage with you in the way they would like. This was a similar theme amongst the professionals I interviewed across the globe.

A Japanese neonatologist shared,

"I always pretend to be constant, not to change my face and tone, so there was no way for the parent to realize the change in my mind and emotions."

When I started my professional clinical career as an Occupational Therapist in the early 1990's, I worked in a rehabilitation center and vividly remember my manager telling me to not get too close to my patients or their families as I would lose or minimize my professional objectivity. He thought that an increased clinician and patient connection would cause me to be a less capable therapist. I struggled with that advice, partly because it did not sit well with my personality or the reason I went into healthcare, and partly because I simply didn't agree with it. While I understood the importance of remaining objective to make sound clinical judgments, I also knew that the more I got to know and connect with my patients and their families, the better therapist I became. I spoke their language, laughed at their jokes, listened to their perspective, and cried alongside them. I believed that staying human kept me connected to the human journey. It still does.

Another way in which vicarious trauma can show up in parents is via other parents. This can happen when you internalize other parents' stories to your detriment.

A British NICU and Special Needs parent of 26-week and 30-week pre-term infants shared:

"I go to parent groups. This is going to sound awful, but I go because there is always someone there who is worse than me, and, occasionally, I need to know that. It is very strange to know that we've got issues, but it could be far worse."

For this mother, hearing more horrific stories than her own allowed her to appreciate her present state.

One thing I ask you to always remember is this:

Trauma is never your fault.

Make this a part of your healing mantra if you choose. From a personal and professional perspective, it is an important distinction to make, message to share, and line to draw for anyone who has experienced trauma. In my coaching practice, I have seen all too often this line getting blurred, leaving people to feel like they were somehow innately responsible for what happened to them.

For NICU, Bereaved, and Special Need parents, there can be significant self-blame that occurs. I understand this type of blame because I experienced it myself, and I was certain that it was my fault my son was born so early, even though my doctors said it was not. I felt equally responsible for my previous and subsequent pregnancy losses. I am not alone. A majority of the parents I interviewed had moments where they felt guilty and responsible for their child's preterm birth.

An American NICU mother of 25-weeker twins shared how she

"had lots of guilt for multiple things"

and continually questioned,

"What did or didn't I do that got us in this situation?"

Several of the professionals I interviewed shared that they also witnessed parents blaming themselves, despite their repeated assurances to them that it was not their fault. Maybe having a reason, even if it's self-blame, is an attempt to make sense of something that is senseless. For some parents, this self-blame aspect of trauma shows up as guilt, and sometimes shame is mixed up in this guilt. This only adds another layer of trauma onto an already traumatic experience.

Interestingly, this guilt-inducing trauma sometimes manifested itself as denial or minimizing of the trauma. Parents felt guilty for even thinking about their experience as traumatic.

One NICU and Special Needs mother from the USA shared,

"I don't like the word trauma or saying that I went through it because it sounds so severe. I had never experienced any real trauma in my life. However, looking back, there's no other way to describe my birth experience or its aftermath."

Or

Another American NICU mother of a 24-week preterm infant shared,

"I was in a lot of physical pain from my emergency C-section, and it was so hideous with the staples up and down, but I dismissed this pain. What I've come to learn about trauma is that I relive that experience of being in pain while seeing my son in the NICU. I can feel it. I can smell it. I can taste it."

In both instances above, the parents were trying to somehow downplay the trauma they were experiencing, but their efforts did not decrease it. There was this notion that they were in some way not experiencing what they defined as real trauma, such as fighting in a war. I can understand this thought process when you consider that, traditionally, trauma was mainly thought and spoken of within the confines of war, natural disasters, abuse situations, etc. This is changing, and increasingly, time spent in the NICU is also being described as traumatic. A National Institute for Health and Care Research (NIHR) study stated that the hospitalization of a person's newborn in a NICU represents a potentially traumatic event for parents, causing increased anxiety and post-traumatic stress. Hence, it is important not to ignore or downplay the trauma that exists in the NICU space, as well as the bereavement and special needs spaces. This increased awareness and acknowledgement can mitigate some of the shame felt and be a part of healing.

The presence of trauma within the NICU, Bereavement, and Special Needs spaces is being increasingly researched, leading to the following emerging outcomes:

NICU and Trauma: The NICU is trauma personified. Recent research has shown that about 40 percent of parents have anxiety or post-traumatic stress when their newborn baby needs intensive care.

One American NICU mother of a full-term baby shared how her post-NICU stress showed up as:

"medical trauma in which I didn't have a doctor's appointment for eight years afterwards. I didn't really connect the dots as to how traumatized I was from all of it. I just sort of pushed it all down and kept saying that I was fine."

Bereavement and Trauma: Parents who lose their child experience a heightened sense of grief and trauma. A study published in National Institutes of Health stated this as well as highlighted the concept of complicated grief. This is defined as prolonged grief that causes a person significant distress many years after the loss. It also showed that "25% of bereaved parents experienced this type of extended or heightened grief versus 10% with a spousal loss and 5% with parent loss." Researchers surmised that "the loss of a child is a loss of traumatic proportions in comparison with other family losses."

Special Needs and Trauma: Although the World Health Organization (WHO) has stated that there is little data on neonatal morbidities worldwide, a study in the UK showed that 76 percent of babies born before 26 weeks gestation had long-term morbidity, such as cerebral palsy, attention-deficit disorders, blindness, deafness, neurosensory impairment, decreased cognition and motor skills, academic difficulties, etc.

When reflecting about the trauma that parents in the NICU, Bereavement, and Special Needs spaces feel, a NICU mother of a 25-weeker from the USA stated,

"It is the kind of experience that makes anyone question every assumption they had about pregnancy, birth, parenthood, life, and death."

As I mentioned before, trauma changes you, preventing you from ever going back to the person you were pre-trauma. The majority of the parents I interviewed expressed this in some way. You can't undo the trauma experience. It has happened, but you can find ways to go through it in a healthy manner. My hope is that walking together through these pages will give you at least one way that makes sense for you.

Within the three parental spaces we're discussing in this book, the concept of trauma-informed care is gaining more traction and recognition. It is defined as a framework or model that recognizes the impact of trauma on people and seeks to provide better care using this increased awareness. It is the backdrop to any intervention, care, or treatment provided, with the person being cared for at the core and the care is compassionate and intentional. This type of care should not only be for the babies but also for the parents and families caring for that baby.

Mary Coughlin, Former Neonatal Nurse, Trauma Informed Expert, author of Trauma-Informed Care in the NICU, and Founder of Caring Essentials Collaborative, sums up the concept in this way:

"It's about rehumanizing the environment [and] cultivating compassion."

In thinking about the clinicians and professionals throughout our emotional and medical journey, the ones I remember fondly have been the ones who showed my family and me kindness and compassion in addition to their technical skill and expertise. The ones who made me feel seen and heard. This reminds me of one of my favorite quotes by the late American poet Maya Angelou, which says: "I've learned that people will forget what you said, people will forget what you did, but people will never forget how you made them feel."

For me, my trauma was minimized when my care was humanized.

A British neonatologist described how she personally practices in a more human way and the power of this in building a stronger physician-parent trust and relationship,

"If the parent is there, they can recognize those subtle differences, so as a doctor, when I go in and see the baby and think they are alright, but the parent says to me, 'I came in yesterday and he was a completely different baby and today he's not himself', I listen. It may not be something you pick up on an observation chart or monitor but it is important, and I would take that more seriously. Even if I don't change what I do in the management of that baby, I may say to the parent, 'You know what? I'm going to come back in an hour and have another look'. I take it seriously because parents are by the cot side a lot more than we are and a lot more than nurses are. The nurses are often looking after more than one baby, but the parents are sitting there watching their baby, watching the monitor. We do say to parents don't look at the monitor but they're observing their baby far more closely and know their baby much more than we will ever know."

Once I saw an image that caught my eye. It was a picture of two dogs, a tall one and a short one, standing in mud. The mud covered the tall dog's ankles and the short dog's whole body. Underneath them was this question: How deep is the mud? and response: Depends on who you ask. If you are like the tall dog, the mud is not that deep, but if you're like the shorter dog, it can feel like quicksand. This is akin to experiencing traumatic events. The depth of life's mud is unique to us, our story and situation, and cannot be compared to anyone else's. Everyone's vantage point differs and is valid.

A Ukrainian NICU mother of a 28-week preterm baby shared,

"We do not have to evaluate who is suffering more."

ANGER

*Anger: A strong feeling of annoyance,
displeasure, or hostility*

Anger. Almost half of the parents I interviewed expressed having feelings of anger at various points along their emotional journey. It is an integral part of the lived experience, so cannot be ignored or minimized.

A Bereaved mother from the USA shared with me that, shortly after her twin boys had died, a family member emailed her saying that

"she hoped I got well soon and next time around, there would be four kids."

When this mother wrote back, expressing her shock and anger, the family member responded that she,

"would not have anything to do with the mother anymore, because she felt [the mother] was overreacting."

This exchange unfortunately was passed to other family members who also categorized her as overreacting. This mother shared with me that she was devastated at her family's behavior and description of her.

Anger, like most emotions, can show up in all kinds of ways, depending on the person and situation, and can have a whole-body impact. Physical symptoms of anger can include clutched fists, flushing or reddened skin, increased heart rate, raised voice, facial frowning, and gritted teeth. Internally, symptoms such as increased heart rate, increased stress, and high blood pressure can show up. Research shows that feeling chronic or repressed anger can also lead to significant mental health challenges such as anxiety and depression and even a shortened life span.

There is a deep level of intensity that encapsulates itself around anger, leading to this emotion sometimes being described as either rage or wrath. It conjures up images of being out of control, irate, uncooperative, unreasonable, volatile, and, in extreme cases, acts of violence.

Due to this emotion being viewed within a negative context, we don't want to be around angry people or be seen as that angry person. So, we try to avoid anger at all costs, or if we do feel it, make every attempt to control it, zip it up, or banish it from our existence all together. Parents I have worked with have shared how they often resist owning or admitting that anger is a part of their lived experience and instead try their hardest to push it as deep down as they possibly can.

A Hungarian NICU and Special Needs mother shared the following experience, which provoked her to feel and suppress her anger.

"When my son turned seventeen, we had to do the paperwork for adulthood because he was intellectually disabled and needed an assessment by an external expert to confirm this. We went to the assessment, and I had to watch him humiliate my son. Although it was obvious that my son had intellectual deficits, he was taking him through things that he knew he could not do. I tried to keep it together, but in my mind, I was thinking, 'You're not going to damage me or see me weak.'"

In this case, she later shared with me how she pushed her true feelings down as a way to protect herself emotionally, which can sometimes be counterproductive. Suppression can provoke an internal, never-ending, and exhausting battle within you.

If you are struggling with or feeling anger, I invite you to free yourself up by viewing and discussing it as being a normal and valid emotion in response to trauma. With that in mind, let us walk through anger together.

When my parenting journey with my husband began in the mid-2000s, I naively thought it would be a breeze. There was no reason for me to think for one moment that it would not be because most of the women in my family seemed to have had this pregnancy and birthing thing down pat. There were a couple of losses in there with some of them, including my mother, which was sad, but these seemed to not be the norm. The women in my family were my measuring stick.

Hence, inspired by the American French dancer, singer, and actress, Josephine Baker, I had always envisioned having ten children, five biological and five adopted. My mother was the oldest of 13; I have three sisters, and growing up, my family was a foster family for more than ten years, so our home seemed to always be filled with children. Although I wasn't the type of person to dream about marriage and babies, I just assumed that if and when it did happen, everything would be like clockwork. I was not emotionally prepared in the slightest when it was not, and this made me angry. There, I said it aloud. I was angry because of:

- Losing four pregnancies, including my son's twin.
- Not being able to complete a full pregnancy, which I know now is called Secondary Infertility.
- Other people's responses to both of the above.
- My son's retinal disease not being caught in time leading to his sight loss, *(This is my personal belief that I cannot prove, but feel deeply)*.

- Other people's treatment of my son as a less capable person because of his blindness, even though he is not.
- Constantly battling systems (e.g., medical, educational, organizational, etc.) to get appropriate understanding, support, and opportunities for my son.
- Not being listened to or believed.

And the list goes on and on. If I'm honest, flashes of annoyance still come up for me sometimes, even now. I desperately try to suppress it.

The impact of this is that we rarely, if ever, win this internal battle. Anger has a strong capacity to fester and spread during our suppression process. The more we try to suppress it, the more it grows, until eventually it rages like a fire burning within us, waiting to burn the next thing or person that happens to cross our path.

This internal burning was shown in the experience of an American Bereaved mother of 20-week twins, who shared,

"About two months after we lost the girls, I had to go to my general practitioner. He asked questions and said, 'Well, we see you have some markers for depression and anxiety. Can you tell me what is going on? Is that from your infertility struggles?' I was like, 'No, it is from my dead babies who are sitting on a shelf in my house.'"

In this story, that doctor was on the fire path of this mother, and he was burned. His obliviousness and failure to read this mother's chart infuriated her so much that the anger flowed out of her through her terse and snide remark.

It is important to remember that anger, just like all these emotions, can and does often come in waves. All the emotions can also be felt simultaneously with one another. I liken it to participating in a ballroom dance with several dance partners. The dance partners are your emotions. In this ballroom, it is common for anger to tango with fear, then move on to do a salsa with guilt, followed by a foxtrot with grief, onto doing a cha-cha-cha with anxiety, and a waltz with sadness. Then repeat with the dance partners and types changing.

To raise awareness with my coaching clients about the interconnectedness of emotions, I sometimes use this Ballroom Dance analogy as a way to intentionally be curious about three things:

- Who are you dancing with? (**Note:** which emotion?)
- What type of dance are you doing? (e.g., slow, fast, simple, complex, or a combo?)
- What, if anything, does it say about you? Your situation?

This increased awareness helps you better understand the emotion itself, how it impacts and shows up in your life, and what other emotions may be tagging along with it. Applying this to this section's emotion, you could ask yourself any or all the questions below as they resonate with you:

- What is anger to you?
- How is anger impacting or showing up in my life?
- What other emotions are tagging along with your anger?

Sitting with whatever your responses are to those questions, without any adjustments or self- judgment, is key to your healing. Although sitting with your anger may not be the easiest or the most comfortable thing to do, acknowledging that it exists helps you to start managing it versus it managing you. Anger must be allowed to exist within our stories because it is a part of them.

A personal example of how anger existed in mine and admittedly managed me was:

During my third pregnancy, after the previous loss of two heartbeats and the extreme premature birth of my son, I started to unfortunately experience the telltale signs that to me by now had unfortunately become familiar, that another loss was imminent. Quickly arranging for our neighbor friends to take care of our toddler son, my husband and I rushed to the hospital. During the drive there, I felt scared and the slow buildup of a lump in my throat as I fought back the stinging tears that had risen to my eyes and were falling down my face. "Not again," I thought, "not again," as I tightly squeezed my husband's hand and silently prayed that this pregnancy could be saved. We were near that erroneously "safe" three-month mark, so it was possible, wasn't it? Desperately clinging to any shred of hope I could find, loads of questions and possibilities raced through my head. Upon arriving at the hospital's emergency room and going through all the initial check-in procedures, I was placed in a room to wait for the doctor. By this time, I was in extreme pain, and the kind nurse had given me painkillers and loads of hospital pads to control the bleeding. After a few minutes that felt like hours, the doctor came in. Without an ounce of compassion and in a quick curt voice, he asked me why I was crying, and in a patronizing tone, asked, "Don't you *know* that you're having a miscarriage?"

My first and totally justifiable response (at least to me) was to wallop him a few times with my fists right then and there. Looking at him incredulously, with my eyes now stinging with both acute anger and extreme sadness all mingled together in my tears, it took every single fiber of my being to keep me and my fists from doing so.

If I wasn't in so much pain, I wouldn't have thought twice about it or its consequences. Please know that I'm not a violent person and don't condone it, but in that moment of uncontrolled and unmanaged anger, it seemed like a perfectly reasonable response and option to consider. In my case, the unmanaged part of it all was that not only was I feeling anger at the doctor for being so aloof, uncaring, and incapable of making professional comments, but somewhere buried deep within all my doctor-focused hostility, I was also angry at my body for failing me yet again. My reasoning was, if it hadn't failed me, I wouldn't be in the company of this awful doctor … nor have to once more say goodbye before I said hello to another baby and pregnancy. Failure means not reaching your potential or not being successful. Hence, for me, my anger was tied to the feeling that I was not a success in this area of my life. I had fallen short of my imagined parenthood, and I did not like it one bit.

If I had been coaching myself all those years ago, I would have encouraged myself to pause and consider the awareness questions above, which I have slightly modified.

- What is anger to me in this moment?
- How is it showing up in my life?
- What other emotions are tagging along with my anger?

By doing so, I would have been better equipped to tap into, expose, and sit with the multi-layered aspects of my anger, including how failure was tied into it. Even if I had not fully known what to do with this emotion, my increased awareness of it would have allowed me to hold space with my anger in a productive way versus giving a right-hook to a doctor.

Several of the parents I interviewed shared their experiences with anger, including:

Anger at:

- **Loss of baby:**

  "Some anger that they wouldn't take him to the NICU and try to save him (second twin born; first was born sleeping). It does make me angry, and yes, that was in 2007 and some of the standards of care have changed since then where they do attempt, but they did not then. They just let him pass on his own."

  (An American Bereaved mother of 22-week preterm twin boys [non-NICU] who both died in the hospital)

- **Own body for not functioning "normally":**

  "This was like my job, and I was sad and angry and separated myself from the world and just stayed there."

  (NICU mother from the USA of a 23-week preterm baby on bedrest in hospital from 19 weeks gestation onward)

- **Parents whose child had an older gestational age and/or shorter NICU stay:**

  "I get really annoyed when people say they had a premature baby at 37 weeks and was in the NICU overnight for observation. I'm like, 'Really?' It just does my head in."

  (A British NICU mom of a 26-week preterm baby who spent one year in the NICU)

- **Other people's responses:**

"[After the] loss of the first baby, I felt invalidated, and there was no one to talk to. After the loss of the second baby, I still felt invalidated, and now I'm angry. Now, I'm like, y'all need to just get out of my face because you want my hurt to fit into your box of what's comfortable for you. You have no idea how I got here because you haven't taken time to ask."

(Bereaved mother from the USA who experienced several pregnancy losses reflecting on her friends' response to her losses)

- **Medical and educational systems:**

"I felt a lot of anger by the time my child got the cerebral palsy diagnosis many years later. There was this entire framework of everybody knew better versus us knowing better."

(An American NICU mother of a 30-week preterm infant sharing how nobody in the systems listened to or took concerns she raised seriously)

- **Not having right information, treatment, or care:**

"I get angry because someone knew. Healthcare professionals somewhere in the world were practicing NIDCAP and infant behavior and reading infant cues and adjusting their care accordingly, and that was not happening in our case. Anger probably supersedes the guilt. That the NIDCAP message isn't being shared everywhere, and so many lives are being adversely affected and altered forever."

(A NICU mother from Ireland of a 25-week preterm baby after learning about the developmental care approach that her child did not receive)

As these examples show, the manifestation of anger is vast, has multiple causes or triggers, and has various recipients, which can include the parents themselves. I wonder if the diversity of anger's origin adds to its perceived uncontrolled nature, with our continuous suppression of it sometimes backfiring, causing its eruption towards anything or anybody.

Anger is simply one of the rawest and truest of all our emotions.

Parents in my coaching practice and the ones I interviewed shared with me that, while anger was an anchor in their emotional journey, they are more likely to discuss other emotions instead of anger. What I often see in my practice is that attempts to ignore or suppress anger are futile. We can try to hide it, but it will eventually rise to the top. One study showed that when we suppress our anger, we, in fact, increase our pain.

In other words, it hurts more to hide.

The story snippets and quotes from parents above show that anger can't be hidden forever. It should not be. It also should not be judged. Due to anger sometimes being directed towards others, this can lead us to self-judge or self-loathe. I've heard parents in my coaching practice say things like "I shouldn't have said that" or "I'm not a good person for thinking or feeling angry." All the other emotions we will explore—guilt, anxiety, overwhelm, grief, shock, and fear—are ones we tend to feel within ourselves. Anger can be felt outside of us and towards other people, which is even more reason to heal from it.

So, what is the next step towards doing this? What lessons can we learn from our anger that we can use as a mechanism to propel us forward? Let's reflect on this further together via the experience of a NICU, Bereaved, and Special Needs mother from Canada I interviewed.

REFLECTION

"I celebrate my child with cerebral palsy (CP) every day. What sucks is that I have to modify my entire house to make it accessible for my son and not know where the money is coming from. We had to buy an accessible van with a lift for him and fight to get extra help for him at home. The system makes me angry because it is like they are fighting against us. I had to fight for one year to get support at home for my son to have a shower as I could no longer do it myself as he is a big boy now, and I pay my taxes. I had to prove that my child needed it when my child has quadriplegic CP and is 100% dependent. So why do I need to prove that he needs assistance all the time? Just come to my house and spend one day, and you will see. I get angry when people use accessible parking spot [when they are not disabled] because that is the only time they want to be in my shoes."

In this mother's world, the system bore the wrath of her anger because it:

- Was financially draining.
- Caused undue stress to her family and son.
- Prevented her son's basic needs being met.
- Did not believe her.
- Questioned her judgment.
- Was a constant antagonist.

If you sit with this mother a little longer, you'll hear something else. Coupled with her system anger, there is also some unspoken internal anger at not being allowed or able to fully celebrate her child due to so much energy being spent trying to fight for him.

Anger mixed with sadness mixed with guilt. I get it. Sometimes I felt the same way too.

If I had coached this mom, I would initiate self-reflection by encouraging her to do one thing:

Simply sit with and notice her emotion of anger.

No judgment. No trying to figure it out. No running from it. Just be.

This is similar to the practice of mindfulness, which means to be fully present with where you are and what you're feeling. I believe there is such power in a pause, and as human beings, we don't often give ourselves this gift. In my coaching practice, it has proven beneficial for my clients to take a pause, so they are more in tune with themselves and can better understand their starting point, before they even take the next step.

I often don't put a timeframe on this pause and reflective phase but let my client decide when they are ready to go further and explore. Returning to the mother above, pausing could have helped her to not carry so many manifestations of her anger at the same time. This can weigh her down and overwhelm her emotionally, while decreasing her clarity to move forward.

EXPLORATION

After reflection, the aim is to facilitate and provoke her to have a deeper awareness of both her expressive and repressive anger by asking exploratory questions such as *(in no particular order and not an exhaustive list):*

1. How is anger present in you?
2. What do you notice about your anger triggers?
3. What does anger give you?
4. What is anger taking from you?
5. What does this say about you, if anything?

Exploring questions like these serves to give us clarity. Clarity of our emotions and clarity of direction. In this mother's case, they could assist her in recognizing her own anger—not anger in general, but what anger truly means and looks like for her and her situation. Remember I mentioned previously about each emotion manifesting itself differently in each person? This is true. Although there may be similarities, your anger won't look, sound, or feel like my anger. It is not supposed to. Realizing this may minimize some of the self-judgment associated with anger and free you to simply feel it in your own way.

All my exploration questions above and throughout this book include some variation of what you want your desired outcome to be for each emotion. This was deliberate to discourage ambiguity and encourage you to be explicit about what you want and need. In the case of this emotion, it helps you create a clear picture of your healed anger destination because how will you know that you've arrived if you don't know what it looks like?

In coaching, we call this evoking awareness, which simply means to facilitate insight. I do this in my practice by prompting and gently challenging my clients to be more transparent and honest about and with themselves.

We discussed earlier our tendency sometimes to squash or hide anger. There is another thing I've noticed parents I've worked with do more with this emotion than others—compartmentalize. Our desire to carefully control our anger may contribute to us trying to keep it separate from our other emotions and ourselves.

Compartmentalization is not always a bad thing if it helps us to hold space and be truly present with only one emotion. Sometimes this is healthy to avoid feeling overwhelmed. Growing up, my mother used to tell my sisters and I, "You can't eat a whole elephant in a day." In my young child's mind, I was initially horrified that she would kill an elephant and try to feed it to us. It took me a moment to realize that she simply meant you can't do everything at once. Sometimes things and situations are just too enormous, like the elephant, for us to tackle them in one go. We must manage it little by little. This is the same with our emotions, especially our anger. Trying to tackle it all at once can burn us. I have met parents in my coaching practice who are so consumed by anger at their journey that they are mad at everything and everyone, without distinction or logic. Their anger is like a concrete block that repels any forward movement.

Revisiting the Hungarian mother who shared her son's assessment experience with us earlier, she described more of her experience.

"Then the expert doing the assessment asked me, 'Did you have any signs during pregnancy that your child "would have problems?"' I was like, excuse me? I tried to keep it together and said to him, 'No, there were no signs at all that he was going to be like this or that I might die in five minutes.' In my mind, I was thinking, 'How dare you ask that question?'"

In this example, the mother separated the anger and annoyance she was feeling so she could get through the assessment process. She chose her words carefully and only chewed a piece of that accusatory elephant in front of her that was in the form of an expert. Although silent, his accusation that she 'must've known something about her child's subsequent "problems", was very loud. This mother's sarcastic, thinly veiled annoyed response was even louder—and in that moment, necessary for her to be present and function in that precise moment.

In moments like these, being still and noticing your discomfort, your feelings, and your thoughts are important in moving you towards healthy processing of your emotions. They provide you with the opportunity and power to choose how or if you want to respond to how you're feeling and/or your situation. In the case above, the mother's internal stillness allowed her to have a quick but powerful internal dialogue that ended with the determination that the anger she was feeling in that situation would not damage her. Anger gave her self-determination, which could lead to her healing.

A NICU mother from the USA used her anger at how she was being treated during her first pregnancy of a 35-week preterm baby in two separate, yet related ways: to advocate for herself during her second pregnancy of a 30-week preterm baby, and to advocate for others within her professional realm. She shared:

"With my first pregnancy, I was a teen mom and almost just a shell that was carrying this baby. Conversations would be directed towards my mother-in-law, Mom, or whoever was accompanying me to the doctor appointments because my husband was away in the military. The majority of the time, it was like I wasn't even in the room. This made me start advocating for myself during my second pregnancy. Professionally as a parent advocate, I gravitated to those younger parents and spent so much time talking to them to let them know, I'm not labeling you because I was labeled."

In each of these scenarios, the parents were able to get something beneficial from this emotion. Their voice, courage, resilience. Let's spend a moment discovering how you can begin to do the same by shifting your anger towards something that is positive, beneficial, and forward-moving for you.

ACTION

One way to do this is to be curious—about yourself. In coaching, this shows up by me facilitating your growth as an individual, in order for you to process and better use or manage your anger. Looking at the parents' experiences above, we can pull back a few more layers and be curious about the following three things:

1. **Your Anger's Impact**: Consider one way you can use the emotion of anger to positively impact how you show up in your future. (e.g., advocacy, self-determination, etc.)

2. **How You Will Use It**: Name one way you will use this impact to move you forward. Notice the subtle difference between my asks of you? Above, I'm inviting you to be curious about what you *can* use, but now I'm asking what you *will* use. Think of the "biting the elephant" concept we discussed earlier.

3. **Support Needed**: What and/or who do you need to help you manage your anger? This question encourages accountability towards yourself and others. Since anger is an emotion that is often felt inward but expressed outward to others, consider using others to help you shift. The only caveat is to make sure it is someone you feel emotionally safe with.

Journaling:

Grab a notebook or piece of paper and write down your answers to the following questions:

1. How does Anger show up for you?
2. What do you want to change about Anger in your life?
3. How will you know when you've achieved it? (i.e. What will you be doing, saying, thinking, or feeling differently than now).

Next, write down any other thoughts that are coming up for you about Anger.

— EMOTION —

ANXIETY

Anxiety: An extreme feeling of worry, unease, or nervousness about something with an uncertain outcome, or feeling excessively apprehensive that something bad or unpleasant is going to happen.

You may have heard people utter the phrase, "I feel anxious," and you may have even said it yourself. Maybe you're in unfamiliar surroundings. Maybe you're about to take an exam. Maybe you're feeling anxious due to something more internal, such as managing a long-term illness.

The American Psychiatric Association states that anxiety is a normal response to stress. They also state that anxiety disorders can be considered the most common mental disorder, affecting almost 30 percent of adults at some point in their lives. There are noted differences between normal anxiety and anxiety that isn't and involves feelings that are excessive around an anticipation of a future concern. In other words, this latter type of anxiety can cause us to experience extreme worrying over what could happen. This sums up my experience in the NICU.

Emotional symptoms of anxiety can range from having difficulty concentrating, feeling tense and on the edge (i.e., panicky), irritability, and a sense of dread. Physically, you may experience heart palpitations, feeling restless, increased sweating, shaking/trembling, nausea, or like you have a "knot" in your stomach. Although I'm separating them out across the physical and emotional lines, anxiety is a whole-body emotion.

These symptoms are similar to the ones experienced with fear, which is also discussed in this book. This is because anxiety and fear are often interlocked due to both emotions serving to alert us to try to prepare our bodies for real or perceived danger. They differ in that anxiety is typically in response to an internal conflict, while fear tends to be a response to an external one. Hence, it's an important to mention again that the emotions we're exploring together do not exist in silos but often overlap with one another.

The impact of anxiety on our bodies and minds is vast. You may feel like you are in a constant state of turmoil in which your thoughts ruminate in your head without an end or solution in sight. During and after my NICU experience, the daily and ongoing uncertainty of being in that space caused anxiety to reign supreme within me. I was frequently worried about the unknowns, and since not knowing is a backbone of the NICU, anxiety could easily have been my middle name. It became such an integral part of how I showed up that I could never truly relax and not worry throughout our whole 5½ months there. Thoughts of what if, if only, could it, will it, and maybe ran through my head continuously.

I felt anxious daily—every time I left the hospital, every time I arrived, and while I was home in between my departure and arrival. In all three instances, my anxiety skyrocketed because of the unknown factor. A palpable feeling of my stomach being completely balled up in knots was a prominent feature. I never knew what to expect and often assumed the worst. When leaving the hospital, I wasn't sure if that would be the last time I saw my son. When arriving, I was not sure if he had made it through the night. While at home, I was nervously waiting for the hospital to ring me to tell me he had not.

It was a horrible way to feel and exist, yet it became my norm. I hid it well, or so I thought, but in hindsight, I didn't. I had surmised that hiding my anxious feelings made me appear strong, but it sapped my strength to its core. I wasn't alone in doing this.

An Irish NICU mother to a 25-week preterm baby described it this way:

"I mask my anxiety, but I'm literally melting inside thinking, 'How am I going to handle this? What's the next thing to get us to a better place?' Outside I'm calm and collected and can engage with whoever I need to, but inside I'm a complete mess."

Not only does anxiety impact our bodies and minds, it also can adversely affect and change our relationships with others, including our spouses, partners, family, and friends. We can become either overly dependent or socially isolated and withdrawn from people around us. Several of the parents I interviewed expressed the latter relationship change. Partly because they felt that nobody really understood what they went and are going through, and partly because of the expectation of others for them to tell their story and the impact of what happens when they do.

One American NICU mother of a 24-week preterm infant shared,

"I still find baby shower invitations challenging, and I don't attend most baby showers, primarily because at those events, a lot of conversations come around about sharing stories. I am still working through being silenced because my story was too dark, too heavy—a conversation-stopper. For example, we were at a toddler gym class after we were finally allowed to take [my son] out. Everyone started telling their baby or birth stories. I was like, 'Oh no, no' [sense of dread]. When it got to my turn, I just skimmed over it really fast and said something like, 'He was preterm; we were in the NICU and here we are'. Someone asked, 'How early was your child?' When I said, 24 weeks 5 days, you could feel the air being sucked out of the room."

It's understandable that being in situations like these only heightens or exacerbates anxious feelings, so are avoided. There is a balance to be had, though, between avoidance to mitigating anxiety and incorporating self-advocacy within that space to combat or control anxiety.

In my coaching practice, two things I remind my clients of as a way of gaining this balance are 1) They own their story, and 2) Their story is theirs to tell—or not. The "or not" is key and where the self-advocacy, which means speaking up for yourself, comes into play. I believe this also means speaking up by either saying no or staying silent. I'm not advocating being impolite or rude, and, of course, you can share your story if you so wish. Equally, if you don't feel ready, able, or even have the desire to share, it is ok to respectfully decline. Doing this gives you some of your power back. For example, I have coached as well as interviewed bereaved parents or parents of multiples in which one or more of their children have died. They all shared with me a common dilemma they face when people ask them the number of children they have and how they feel conflicted about what their response should be. If they had triplets and one died, do they say they have three children or two? If they have lost all their babies, can any of these be counted? My perspective is that it is their story; they own it, and they can choose to answer or not, in whatever way they choose. They can feel free to set their own boundaries, however they feel is right for them. Clients have shared that being aware of this choice and knowing it is at their disposal decreases their anxiety and increases their sense of control.

Anxiety, like most emotions, is not static or a one-time occurrence but is dynamic and can continue for years and throughout different phases of your life. Even now, although not quite as acute, anxiety can still rear up its ugly head within me because there remains a lot of uncertainty around my son due to his vision loss. The same what ifs and maybes pop up and say hello to me from time to time. I try not to say hello back.

Let's look at how anxiety can have pervasive and long-term effects through the experience of one NICU mother from the USA of 26-week preterm twins whose anxiety continued for over 20 years after the birth of her twins. She shared different manifestations of her anxiety in the following way:

[Shortly after leaving the NICU]

"I had two severely fragile children and a 3rd child who was a toddler at home. I was just working on getting through every day, making sure they were at physical therapy, their follow-up appointments, etc. I was on the hamster wheel and could not get off it. When I did get off it and sat still, then my anxiety levels went up."

[20+ years post-NICU]

"All of those panicky feelings come right back when something happens to my children and they're not right. When my child broke her arm or was in the car accident, or if anything happens to her, it emotionally triggers me because she was so sick and fragile. I get so worried. If something happens to my children, I can barely handle it. I have to really breathe through it and remind myself that we're not back in the NICU. It may be just a broken arm, or I have to take them to the doctor. I don't get triggered when they have emotional issues, only when something physical happens."

When asked what she felt caused her to separate the emotional and physical, she responded:

"Because I feel more equipped to help them emotionally, as most of their emotional issues are a normal part of life that I've already navigated, and they'll just have to learn how to navigate it better. It's no big deal, but physical stuff gives me that 'out of control, I can't fix my preemie' feeling again, and I get really anxious."

This story highlights the longevity of anxiety and how it can manifest itself long after the initial event occurs, even years later. It also shows the importance of knowing what you are experiencing. For example, this mother knew that her anxiety was from her children's physical challenges versus their emotional ones. Identifying what something is helps you to take a step back, even if it's a baby step, to try and assess the situation and decide what to do about it. It can also make it less scary.

This reminds me of when I was a little kid and 100% convinced that a monster resided under my bed, waiting to scare me once the lights were turned off and the room was dark. Of course, I had no actual evidence except my anxious and nervous feelings, which in my mind validated everything. I was also convinced because my hand had accidentally brushed against it one night while I was falling off to sleep. Mustering up the courage to run and turn on the lights, I discovered that my "monster" was actually my furry slippers. Once I'd identified what it was, I immediately felt better and more in control. I'm not comparing or mitigating the anxiety you feel with flurry slippers but am simply highlighting the power of identifying what you're dealing with. The mother, who was experiencing anxiety for 20+ years, knew what was happening to her, identified it, and took steps to help herself get through and be more in control of the moment by *"breathing through it."*

As mentioned previously, anxiety is triggered by the not knowing and uncertainty of situations. It can also be due to you experiencing a situation that you don't want to repeat, such as loss. Bereaved parents I've interviewed discussed this aspect of anxiety. Losing their child or children understandably increased their anxiety and fear of it happening again.

A NICU and Bereaved mother from the USA of 23-week preterm twin boys in which one survived and one did not described the increased anxiousness she felt after her son's death and the subsequent pregnancy with her daughter.

"I had no anxiety before the boys were born. After my daughter was born, I did not sleep and was literally losing myself because I was so worried that something would happen to her."

Now that we know more about anxiety, what it is, its impact, and its different manifestations in the lives of parents who have experienced trauma along their parenting journey, what do we do about it? What can you do?

REFLECTION

Anxiety can perpetuate anxiety, meaning one type can feed off another if not managed. Therefore, it is important to mitigate this by proactively becoming more in tune with the emotion itself versus merely reacting to it.

When working with my coaching clients, I often invite them to pause when there's an emotion bubbling up. I remember having a client who was typically very effusive and always made direct eye contact, start to speak slower and look down and away from me when discussing a particular subject. After further inquiry and conversation, I began to recognize that these behavior changes were signals of her increased anxiety, because slowing down increased her awareness and apparent discomfort with the topic.

I encourage an embracing of this awareness and discomfort. This is because when we pause and become curious about what is really happening with the emotions we feel in our bodies, we're better able to hone in on how and where it is happening within our bodies. This heightened sense of awareness gives us useful information about our internal space and state of being that we can use for our future benefit. For example, for my client I was curious to uncover what it was about that subject which caused discomfort and where in her body she felt it the most. This technique is known as mindfulness, which is the art of pausing and being fully present with yourself without judgment. Being mindful gives you three gifts:

1. Increased awareness,
2. Clarity, and
3. Permission to just be.

I include it in the reflection phase because this pausing can facilitate deep breathing, which according to several studies, has been proven to decrease anxiety. People who are anxious tend to breathe faster, which can increase anxiety, so pausing and deep breathing change the dynamics of this in a healthier manner.

Pausing and being mindful doesn't remove this uncertainty, but it can give you clarity, control, and choice about your response to it. You can choose how you show up and interact with it or not. As I mentioned earlier, a favorite mantra of mine is "There's power in the pause."

A leading UK Bereavement support charity, Cruse, recommends a structured technique of pausing and being present when anxiety strikes. They call it the 5-4-3-2-1. This involves you naming:

- Five things you can see
- Four things you can touch
- Three things you can hear (can include your breathing)

- Two things you can smell
- One thing you can taste

Becoming more aware of yourself and your surroundings in this way taps into your parasympathetic nervous system, which is the system responsible for relaxing our bodies after it experiences stress or danger. It kicks in when we know we feel safe and has some of the following signs:

1. More relaxed breathing
2. Relaxed body posture (not tense)
3. Normal heart rate
4. Normal skin tone (i.e., skin is not flushed)

It also allows you to engage in and emotionally respond to your situation in a calmer and more regulated manner. It is important to note that being regulated does not mean being rigid. In fact, the latter may be a sign of increased anxiety.

One NICU and Special Needs mother of 25-week preterm twins from the USA described her anxiety-filled rigid routine when her children were in the hospital in this way:

"I was trying to grasp at having control in an uncontrollable space. I didn't recognize it at the time, but I created such a regimented schedule of what every day was going to look like. I would wake up in the morning, give my two-year-old son his breakfast, play with him, and put him down for his nap. Then I would go to the NICU, hold one twin for a certain amount of time, and then hold the other one for a certain amount of time. I would pump, and then I had to go home because I had to give my son his dinner, read to him, and tuck him into bed. I had to do it, nobody else. I did all of that because that was all I could control."

This mother had created a very rigid routine in an attempt to be in control, but in the end, she was out of control. She later expressed feeling powerless and how her routine was exhausting and unsustainable. If I were coaching her during that time, I would invite her to tap into her natural internal resource within her nervous system, as mentioned earlier, to gain some of that control back. Let's reflect on a few ways of doing this.

When an emotion showing up in my clients' lives is causing them to feel stuck, I often ask them either one or both of the following questions:

1. What is grabbing your attention about _____ (the emotion)?

2. What is _____ (the emotion) giving you?

I will repeat the questions here and insert the emotion anxiety:

1. What is grabbing your attention about your anxiety?

2. What is anxiety giving you?

You will hear me ask some form of that last question in all the emotion sections. It can appear to be an odd question and usually throws people off track a bit because we don't often think about what an emotion gives us, especially an emotion that we may think of negatively. But emotions do give us something, even if we are not conscious of it. Perhaps it gives you your identity, and you are known as that anxious person. Maybe it gives you a reason to avoid others and situations. Possibly it gives you an invisible badge of honor of sorts to show that you survived trauma.

Consider an American NICU mom to two preterm babies, 33 and 36 weeks. She and her husband both worked full-time, and she also ran a charity. In addition, she was the main caregiver of her father, who had suffered a life-changing illness. Prior to this illness, her father helped her and her family with most things.

Through our discussion, she realized something unexpected she was receiving from anxiety. She shared:

"My father's illness rocked my whole world. He was my right hand with everything, including my charity. I had my regular job and would get my kids off the bus. I moved him in with us after his rehabilitation stay because I was thinking I'm just going to do it all: keep working, take care of the kids, lift this 350 pound man in the bed by myself, etc. To be fair, I did it for three years, but six months into him living with us, the kid's medical issues related to their prematurity became worse. My dad also had another medical issue. Two of the issues happened on the same day within the same hour, and I basically had a panic attack at work. I had no idea and didn't know I had anxiety. I called a therapist, and during our 1ˢᵗ session, I just sobbed."

Upon further discussion of us being really curious about what she was feeling and what was happening, she said:

"I was high-functioning and filling my day with doing all these tasks because I didn't want to feel anxiety. I juggle it all because it appeases my anxiety."

Ah, there it is: appeasement. This is the gift she was getting from anxiety—appeasement. It allowed her to placate and pretend that she was handling it all internally and externally, when in reality, she was not. This highlights another way in which anxiety can negatively impact a person's life, which is through avoidance. To prevent feeling or acknowledging anxious feelings, people avoid them. Avoiding anxiety by filling your life with a bunch of tasks was demonstrated in the mother mentioned above. She was compounding this by compartmentalizing each aspect of her life, meticulously separating or dividing things into different sections to try and manage them all. In a way, her efforts to not feel anxiety were counterintuitive because, through her division and avoidance of this emotion, she was feeling even more anxious. A little piece of anxiety was present in each slice of her life and every task she juggled.

EXPLORATION

How do you heal from anxiety? Prevent it from being your default mode? Before you answer that, consider how you want to heal. I call this your desired outcome. You must know what you want in order to realize when you have it. Thinking along those lines, be curious and honest with yourself when considering the following question:

What is your desired outcome with anxiety?

After you know the outcome you want, consider this question:

What would you be doing, saying, and thinking differently about anxiety that you are not doing now?

Continuing with the appeasement receiving NICU mother above, she answered this question by getting real with herself and her situation and realizing both her limitations and strength. After further inquiry and exploration, she stated:

> *"I just went from one major crisis to the next until I hit my limit and needed to realize that I'd taken on way too much. That it was ok to feel the anxiety and grief of that and not blame myself. It's ok to not do for everyone. I needed to hear this and allow myself to feel it."*

Here are a few ways she showed up differently:

- She became stronger through showing her vulnerability in knowing when she was reaching her limit and by setting boundaries.
- She gained more clarity when she allowed herself to feel her anxiety.
- She carried more, in a healthier way, when she put other things down, despite admitting it was a difficult choice to do less.
- She freed herself up emotionally when she stopped the self-blame and realized her physical and mental health were important, and it was ok to say no.

Doing this was not easy, and she shared that she "still struggles" with it sometimes, but equally she valued her emotional health and knew that anxiety and panic attacks were not the way she wanted to show up in this world as a person, parent, spouse, or daughter.

One of the most powerful things in this mother's example above is the "allowing to feel" part. Throughout this book, I don't want you to run away from or avoid feeling the emotions we're discussing and try to lock them far away in the "emotions to avoid" cupboard and throw away the key. To the contrary, it's important that you feel them and understand what they feel and look like for you. How they show up for you in your life. This is that awareness piece again. Once you know this, you're better able to deal with and manage it. Running from your emotions only makes them appear bigger and feel insurmountable.

ACTION

There are two strategies I invite you to consider to better manage your anxiety in a proactive and healthier way: Deep Breathing, which I've mentioned earlier in this section, and Awareness Building. These may not sound like earth-shattering solutions, yet I frequently use them in my coaching practice in different ways, and they work.

Deep Breathing (2-steps) This is not just regular breathing but deep, slow, diaphragmatic (i.e., from your diaphragm) breathing. The first step is to inhale, taking deep, slow breaths using your diaphragm and slowly count to five. The second step is to exhale your breath as you count to five, making sure your breathing is even slower as you count. Repeat this type of breathing between 5–7 times. Some people choose to close their eyes during it to help them focus more. This type of controlled and purposeful breathing engages your parasympathetic nervous system we discussed earlier, which shuts off the "fight or flight" panicky response and makes us calmer, more engaged, and controlled. This is the type of response you want to counteract an emotion like anxiety.

I often incorporate this type of breathing at the start of the coaching session with my clients, with permission of course, as a grounding technique to help them prepare for our time together and release any potential barriers or distractions.

Awareness Building This strategy is about understanding your beliefs about an emotion and how it shows up in your life. It is based on having an honest, curious inquiry with yourself. When using this with my clients, I use it as part of a bigger strategy around uncovering limiting beliefs. For the purposes of our time together here, I am incorporating the first five questions which focus on raising your awareness. They are intentionally written to be asked in the first person. Please note, I strongly encourage you to jot down the first thing that comes to your mind and not mentally edit your response. I ask this because usually your initial response is the rawest and most authentic.

- How do I know that I am anxious?
- Who is telling me that I am anxious?
- What would I be feeling, seeing, or hearing if I were not anxious?
- In what areas of my life do I feel like I am *not* anxious?
- What's different in those areas of my life where I don't feel anxious?

Journaling:

Ready? Grab a notebook or piece of paper and write down your answers to the following questions:

1. How does Anxiety show up for you?
2. What do you want to change about Anxiety in your life?
3. How will you know when you've achieved it? (i.e. What will you be doing, saying, thinking, or feeling differently than now). **Note:** This question was also asked in the Exploration section above to increase awareness but is intentionally repeated here to promote action.

Write down any other thoughts that are coming up for you about Anxiety.

— EMOTION —

FEAR

Fear: An unpleasant feeling or thought caused by the threat of danger, pain, or harm.

Fear is a primal feeling that serves to protect us from danger by kickstarting a small but powerful part of our brain called the amygdala. Doctors recognize the amygdala as being a major center for processing emotions. It activates the "flight or fight" mechanism. In the anxiety section, I talked about how the anxiety and fear emotions have similar symptoms that trigger this response mechanism.

When experiencing fear, people perceive an external danger or threat, causing this response to occur automatically. Your brain takes over and pumps a load of stress hormones throughout your body to prepare it for action. This is often called the "amygdala hijack" which I shared in more detail with you when discussing trauma earlier. For now, a simple example of this mechanism at work when fear is felt is this: If you're facing that big grizzly bear in the forest, do you stand your ground and "fight" it (hope not) or do you take "flight" and run away as fast as your legs can take you? Likewise, when that big ole grizzly is the emotion in your head and heart, the same thing happens—you either face it or run away. This can be considered a positive aspect of fear for some people because it gives you a choice and provokes you to respond in one way or the other. Fear can cause you to freeze, stop dead in your tracks, and just stay there … perhaps forever. There is no "choice" in this response. This can be one of the many impacts of fear. One parent described fear as feeling "petrified," and another shared that she experienced "extreme fear" at the prospect of having a preterm baby.

As I mentioned in the Introduction, NICU, Bereaved, and Special Needs parents have often had multiple parenting experiences, from infertility to the grave and everything in between, and all these experiences can increase their fear. This is what happened to an American NICU mother of a 24-week preterm infant I interviewed interviewed who had experienced infertility and bereavement prior to her NICU journey. She shared how these prior experiences only served to heighten her fear, pre-, during-, and post-NICU, describing it in this way:

"For me, it started through the infertility journey, where my first pregnancy I lost due to a ruptured ectopic pregnancy, so the fear started immediately. Since it was life-threatening for me, fear started way back there and then continued into the next pregnancy, with the fear of losing another child, and in the NICU, the fear of still losing him and not being able to take him home. Then after [the NICU] and coming home, it's the fear of what's going to happen to him long-term? What will his life look like; will he be able to have a life that he can enjoy; will he have health challenges; is he going to have trouble in school? There are so many unknowns, so it's just the fear of what his life is going to look like, and will he be happy?"

Let's take a deeper look into both the potential physical and emotional impacts of fear.

The phrase "crippled with fear," which perhaps you may have uttered yourself, is often used to describe feeling overpowered and/or paralyzed, rendering you unable to do anything. This relates to that "freezing" I mentioned earlier. Many NICU, Bereaved, and Special Needs parents I've worked with or interviewed have expressed experiencing this due to the "fear of the unknown" that innately comes with their lived experiences in these spaces. In that moment, they simply don't know what to do, say, think, or feel.

Physically, fear can cause you to have the following symptoms:

- Racing heartbeat
- Increased sweat production
- Tightening and/or tingling of your muscles
- Stomach churning
- Light-headedness or feeling faint/dizzy
- Shallow and/or difficulty breathing

Emotionally, you may experience feeling:

- Overwhelmed (refer to that emotion section)
- Out of control
- Sense of impending disaster, doom, or death
- Continuous upset
- Increasing anxiety (refer to that emotion section)

Fear can manifest itself differently with each individual and each situation. The Mayo Clinic and studies on fear published in the National Institutes of Health (NIH), show that the symptoms listed above are common ones experienced by most people. As mentioned previously, for many parents, fear can and often does happen alongside, alternatively, or intertangled with other emotions. This goes back to the rollercoaster element for parents in these spaces in that you feel emotionally unready for feelings that rapidly lunge you forward into an unknown world. Due to the complexity, unexpectedness, and uncertainty of it all, the sense of danger can feel even more intense, causing the amygdala to go into overdrive. NICU and Special Needs parents often state they are both fearful of and anticipating the "what next," that it can sometimes feel like they are walking on eggshells just waiting for the next bomb to drop.

This eggshell-walking showed up for one American NICU and Bereaved mother of a 24-week preterm infant who lived and a 20-week preterm infant who died, in the following way:

"I constantly thought of the 'what ifs' and felt 'intense fear and anxiety' when my son was in the NICU. This unleashed a torrent of questions in my mind that were all based in the fear of what could happen next. Some of my recurring thoughts I had during that time were, 'What could happen to him?; What will his future hold?; What are the consequences of his early birth that he could have for the rest of his life?; Am I even capable of handling these consequences?; Am I equipped to deal with whatever was ahead without knowing what that would be?; Would he even make it out of the NICU?' I had so much fear and anxiety over the future."

This mother had difficulty living in the present because fear had made her so worried about the future. I get it.

During our initial two months in the NICU, our son seemed to constantly hover between life and death. It felt like this because one second, he was stable and the next he'd "coded," which is the medical term for when a person's heart or breathing stops. This prompted the doctors and nurses to race to his incubator to "bring him back." The first time I heard this phrase, I remember thinking, "Bring him back from where?" My brain couldn't and wouldn't register that his life was on the brink of existence and that this is where they were desperately trying to bring him back from before he toppled over for good and didn't exist. Each time it happened didn't get any easier. It got worse because I was now keenly aware that each time he coded, death was near, and each time, I became increasingly fearful that death would "win." This made perfect sense to me because death had won with my son's twin and my other pregnancies. In addition, by being in the NICU, I was repeatedly surrounded by death winning with so many precious babies who are no longer here. I remember each of them and their families to this day.

The first time I experienced one of my son's coding episodes is seared in my brain. I'd just arrived at the NICU for the day and was chatting away with his nurse right outside his NICU bay about how he was doing. She was sharing with me how much better he was getting and how stable he was. It seemed like as soon as the word stable exited her mouth, his alarms started screeching. She stopped in mid-sentence, turned, and raced to him, with her medical teammates right on her heels. I was left in the hallway frozen. I honestly don't even remember moving but do remember my heartbeat sounding so loud in my ear, my pulse racing, and a strong sense of dread. It seemed like hours of me standing there alone, although it was probably only minutes. However long it was, I vividly remember trying to imprint my son's face into my brain so I wouldn't forget what he looked like. His wispy hair, tiny arms that my wedding ring could easily encircle, his big almond-shaped eyes, and his chipmunk cheeks that seemed way too big for his small, perfectly shaped head. I intentionally did not imprint the multiple tubes, oxygen, and equipment he had strapped to him but rather took a mental picture of the parts of him that made him my child. Human. Not patient or statistic.

I did this because I was 100% convinced that my "what next" from the doctors and nurses was going to be "I'm sorry, Gigi; we did all we could but …" I was certain of this, and fear solidified it for me. I was standing directly outside the NICU doors, and although I couldn't see my son, I saw the nurses and doctors around his incubator feverishly working on him. Each time another doctor was called, and they rushed past me to his incubator, my heart sank a little lower. Finally, one of the main consultants (i.e. attending physicians), ran past me to him, and I was convinced that my son had passed away. I thought, "Why else would they need her amongst what appeared to be a large army of nurses and doctors already there?" My heart felt like it had leaped to both my chest and ears and was beating hard, fast, and loud, and I felt such a deep sense of dread. Seconds felt like minutes, and minutes like hours. I didn't even realize that I wasn't breathing until I felt his nurse beside me gently telling me that they'd managed to stabilize him, and I could go in and see and talk to him. Where had she come from? I was so frozen and lost in my state of fear that I did not even see her come out of the NICU door towards me. I finally exhaled as I walked through the NICU doors to see my son.

Even to this day, many moons later, if I get an unexpected call from my son's school or his doctor, in that split second of me reaching to answer the phone, my pulse races and breathing stops. My fear and anticipation of the "what next" still exists. It doesn't go away with time but manifests itself in a different way.

I did not make the connection between my rapid heartbeat at a telephone call and my NICU experience until recently. Oh, I noticed something was happening but did not realize the connection or relationship between my past and present parenting experiences was rooted in fear. I just brushed it off as me being overly sensitive. We will explore how this connection potentially shows up in your life in the Reflections at the end of this section.

For one NICU and Special Needs mother from the USA, her fear-induced parenting showed up in her striving to reach perfection. Her child was born at 30 weeks and subsequently went on to be diagnosed with a range of different special needs, which made her a strong advocate for her child. Despite this, her fear of what could happen was strong and produced a continuous feeling of nervous jitters while she masked her emotions. She explained her fear mindset in this way.

"I was trying to be the perfect mother both in the NICU and years later as I navigated the special needs world. I became a fierce advocate for my child. In the NICU, I was very good at masking my emotions and was afraid to cry because I thought they were going to take my baby away from me. I remember someone telling me that had happened to another mother, so it was in my head all throughout our NICU stay."

Later, after her child was diagnosed with different special needs, she continued:

"Anything 'normal,' I was nervous about. I was also nervous about what was ahead for my child—will she walk, talk? I was trying to be a good mom and continued wearing my mask."

Despite this mother further expressing how physically and mentally exhausting it was to hide how she was really feeling, her fear of what would happen if she did share them caused her to continue to hide them.

Going back to the amygdala we mentioned earlier, one of the things important to mention here is that this structure in our brain is a part of our limbic system, which is responsible for regulating our emotions to ensure our survival. In the mother's case above, one of the ways in which her fear was being regulated was by her hiding it. Of course, hiding any emotion is not sustainable or healthy, but during that moment of time, it ensured this mother's survival to get through what she was experiencing. Another way the amygdala does this is by tapping into your unconscious memory to help you remember things you've learned in the past. Just like you remembering how to ride a bike many, many years after you initially learned how to do it, with fear, your brain reminds you of how you have dealt with fear in the past. If you faced fearful situations head on before, you are more likely to do this again as a NICU, Bereaved, or Special Needs parent. On the other hand, if fear stopped you in your tracks previously, it will continue to do so. There is no value judgment with the amygdala or limbic system, meaning that it is not designed to tell you if your previous response to fear was right or not. It simply taps into what you did before as a guide to what you do now.

Your brain and the limbic system are simply doing what they are designed to do—storing up all your emotional experiences so you can tap into them later. However, when your stored experiences are negative or full of fear, this is not what you want to tap into to help you heal or move forward. One NICU mother of a 25-week preterm infant from the USA shared how her built-in fear of anything medically related played into how she responded to her daughter:

"I felt so terrified of her, of everything medical. When they started talking about her going home soon, I was like, 'Whose home? You'd better not be talking about my home because I'm not a nurse.' What are they talking about? My daughter had an ostomy, which was supposed to be repaired before she came home; she was turning blue when she was feeding. You've got to be kidding me. I was like, 'You've chosen the wrong mom, the wrong person, like no, no, no.'"

Let me clarify that this mother shared that she deeply loved her child and went on to learn to care for and raise her very well, but she was *"terrified"* at first. Her initial response above shows you the automatic connections and sometimes disconnections that can take over when fear is in the driver's seat.

There is an acronym used to describe fear which I often heard repeated in the coaching and self-help spaces. It is:

F — False
E — Evidence
A — Appearing
R — Real

It can be used to explain how fear can sometimes be a self-generated response because, even when we have no idea what is going to happen in the future, we're already afraid of it. For the mother mentioned above, her false evidence appearing real was that she was convinced that she was not equipped or capable of caring for her child because she was not a nurse. In her mind only nurses were able to provide the care she needed.

I can understand this fearful response, especially for NICU, Bereaved, or Special Needs parents. This is because, throughout the course of our journey, many of us have been given so much "doom and gloom" information from professional experts about what our child won't be able to do or what we should accept or expect as a parent that, over time, you start to believe this "evidence" even if it doesn't come true. Similar to the mother's response we've just seen. In a weird way, we're being taught to be fearful while at the same time being told not to be.

On the flip side, the F.E.A.R. acronym can be used in a positive way by assisting us in being a bit more cautious about believing, expecting, and being afraid of the worst before and/or if it even occurs. It can do this by making us examine the "evidence" we use to determine if it is true or not. If it's not, which my years of coaching experience tells me most times is the likely scenario, then let go of your fear.

REFLECTION

In this Reflection section, we will begin to learn how you can start to either release your grip on fear or release fear's grip on you. These are really two sides of the same coin and depend on your perspective: either you hold onto fear or allow fear to hold onto you.

A Canadian NICU and Bereaved mother of 26-week preterm infants in which one lived and the other did not, described how fear gripped her. She shared the following about how fear showed up for her shortly after her son had died:

"I had a lot of fear of losing my surviving son too. On the second day, the doctor came in to give me an update on him and said my son had a heart condition called Patent Ductus Arteriosus (PDA), and I just started crying. He asked me, 'Why are you crying?' I said, 'I've just lost a baby from a heart condition, and now you are telling me that my [living child] also has a heart condition.' So, I cut the doctor off as I couldn't handle any more news."

For this mother, her fear was twofold: fear of losing her surviving child and fear of information. More precisely, the fear of dreaded and unwelcome information.

Reflecting on her fear in that moment, I was curious about two things:

- What was she receiving from her fear?
- What did she want to receive instead? (her desired outcome)

As mentioned in the Anxiety section, I know that we don't typically stop to think about what fear, or any emotion, is giving us, but emotions do give us something, even the emotions we try to rid ourselves of. If we take the emotion of fear, it can give us identity (i.e., "I am a fearful person.") or a tribe (i.e., other people who are also fearful). Other times it can give us a crutch (i.e., "I can't because I'm afraid.").

This may sound like an oversimplification of a deep emotion or that I'm trivializing it, which is not my intention at all. Rather, it is to make you more aware of the emotion of fear and what you may be receiving from it. This increased awareness, or what I like to call your "aha" moments, is key because it does two things:

1. It lets you know that something is there. You won't be able to address fear if you are not aware that it even exists in your life, and

2. It aids you in identifying what fear is in your life and how it is showing up. Increased awareness of the emotion of fear in your life does not mean increased judgment. In fact, I often tell my clients to leave their judgment, especially self-judgment, at the door.

Back to the mother from Canada. When I invited her to reflect on the two questions of what fear gave her and what she wanted to receive from this emotion instead, we found out:

- Fear was giving her protection. In this case protection from bad news, and it allowed her to shut out any unwanted or potentially scary information, and

- She wanted *"to change her son's diaper."* Huh? You may be wondering what in the world does diaper changing have to do with fear or what she wanted to receive. In a nutshell, everything. You see, after continued discussion, observation, and inquiry while giving her space for further reflection, diaper changing symbolically meant something else to her. Her "aha" moment answer of *"I want to be present"* was simple yet profound. Being present for her living child meant being fully there, mentally, emotionally, and physically—for his diaper changes, feeds, rounds, etc.

Upon further reflection, she identified that being present was what she really wanted. Interestingly, she received this via the very thing she tried to avoid—bad information. The more information she knew increased her ability to be present and was no longer the big monster she thought it would be. This is how she described moving from fear to presence:

"About a week later of me shutting down any information, another doctor came in and told me, 'He's your son, and you have a right to know.' He sat down by my bedside and drew a picture of the heart and explained PDA to me like I was a kindergartener, and that changed things for me. I felt I could start to take little bits of information at a time. My transformation from fear to staying present with my son started to happen after that. It gave me the opportunity to be present in the NICU and to learn to be in the now."

- I invite you to reflect on your own fear by considering the following: What is your fear giving you? Your answer to this increases your awareness or "aha" moment, of this emotion in your life.

  What do you want to receive from fear instead? This helps you identify your desired outcome of what you would like to gain from this emotion.

EXPLORATION

We all have the power to shift, change, and alter the trajectory of our emotions and how they show up in our lives. Control means having the power to influence or direct people's behavior or course of events. Looking at fear as an example, you get to define how, when, and where it shows up in your life. Even if it shows up unexpectedly, that's totally ok because you still can have the power to control it versus becoming consumed by it.

How can you start shifting the way you view, control, and navigate fear within your life? You can use your brain in a different way via tapping into its neuroplasticity. This is a big old medical jargon of a word that simply means the brain's ability to change and rewire itself. Plasticity means the ability to be altered, shaped, or molded. Hence, neuroplasticity is the unique way in which the neural networks and pathways in our brain can be altered by changing, growing, and reorganizing itself in response to an experience we have. These experiences can be physical or emotional.

As a former Occupational Therapist specializing in neurology, I spent many years working with people who were battling a range of neurological conditions, such as traumatic brain injury, stroke, brain cancer, Parkinson's disease, spinal cord injury, etc. I repeatedly saw and was in awe of the power of the brain's neuroplasticity. For example, a person who had a stroke would improve their speech, ability to walk, or use of their affected arm via rewiring the messages being sent to the brain. As part of their rehabilitation, our therapy treatment interventions would focus on capitalizing on this natural phenomenon by providing treatment aimed at getting the brain to make new connections that would help them better control the parts of their body that were affected. Although this isn't a neurology book, I feel that it is useful to understand the built-in power and resources we have within ourselves to face and mitigate challenges in our lives. Neuroplasticity is one resource we have at our disposal to use.

We have discussed how neuroplasticity can help us from a physical perspective, but let's explore how it can help us with our emotions. Have you ever taken a walk in a park on the official paved pathways? As you walk on this official path, have you also ever noticed other paths deviating off from the official one? Someone has walked through the grass as a shortcut, perhaps because it was more fun, perhaps because they were simply rebelling from the norm.

In any event, after that first person deviated, another person did, then another, and another, until, pretty soon, you had a completely different path that's been created. Well, a similar thing happens with emotional neuroplasticity—you reroute your typical emotional response and create a new and different one. This is what I invite, encourage, and facilitate my clients to do in my coaching practice, and what I will be inviting you to consider doing with your fear.

James Garrett, a scientist, coach, and founder of Brain by Design, shared a story about his young daughter which highlights how we can reroute or change our emotional response to fear incrementally, step-by-step. He described her re-routing experience in this way:

One day he and his daughter were walking in the park, and a bug started crawling on his daughter's clothes. She began screaming because she thought all bugs were bad and scary. In her mind and based on her reaction, all bugs were the same; hence, her reaction was the same towards every bug. James gently removed the bug from her clothing, allowed it to crawl on his finger, and held it close to him. Removal – This was her 1st reroute. Through the help of her father, she was able to remove or detach herself from her source of fear. When he noticed his daughter had stopped screaming and was curious, with her permission, he moved the bug closer to her. Curiosity was now her 2nd rerouting step. This shift in her emotional response from being fearful to being curious. She stared at the bug on his hand, intensely watching how it moved, its different colors, etc., and this became her 3rd step to rerouting, which was Observation. Facing, the 4th rerouting step of her fear decreasing soon followed as she stepped closer towards the bug, facing it head on. Eventually, she asked her father if she could hold the bug on her own finger, which was her 5th rerouting step of Control. Her ability to take control of the thing she was initially afraid of in the manner she wanted, helped to further decrease her fear. All of this propelled her onto her 6th and final rerouting step, which was Confidence, when she held the bug on her finger. She was assured, confident, and no longer afraid of all bugs.

Her re-routing experience took her from Fear to Confidence. From her initial feeling that all bugs are bad to maybe perhaps some are not. The change in his daughter's perception and emotional response about bugs didn't occur immediately but was done step-by-step. It is the same with you.

To change or re-route the way you view, manifest, and respond to fear in a way that moves you forward instead of holding you back, you have to alter your reaction or response to it little by little. This is how you create those new paths of a different emotional response to fear. Research shows that it takes on average 66 days, which is approximately two months, for a new habit or change to form. Hence, fear won't disappear overnight but you must intentionally re-route how you view and respond to it one step at a time.

Notice that I didn't say you must alter the emotion itself, as the emotion is what it is. Fear is fear, guilt is guilt, etc. You will feel them. We all do. Rather, it is how you respond when you feel them. What you do, say, think. That's the shift and change I'm inviting you to consider here.

In the Preface, we discussed the concepts of compartmentalization and processing. The former being all about keeping things separate or isolated, and the latter about keeping things together. Let's take a closer look at fear through the lens of these two concepts as a way of you starting your re-routing process with this emotion.

Consider the following questions. You don't need to answer them all but choose a few that resonate with you.

- What does fear or being fearful look and/or feel like for you?
- When do you experience fear the most?
- When do you fear the least?
- How often do you embrace fear?
- How do you express fear?
- In what ways is fear silent in your life?

- Think of a time when you faced your fears. Describe what happened.
- How is fear intertwining with other emotions you experience?

If you found it difficult to answer most of the above questions, you may be compartmentalizing fear more than you realize. Unconsciously slicing it up into tiny bits of your life that you can't even recognize it. When trying to describe an emotion you are feeling, have you said things like, "I feel it but can't put my finger on it." If you've heard yourself say this, then you may need a bit more clarity and awareness around how fear is manifesting itself within your psyche.

Fear becomes bigger when you can't or don't recognize it within yourself.

This can be manifested when you find yourself scared of anything and everything, regardless of whether it is justified or not. This is what happened to an American NICU mother of a 23-week preterm infant, who shared:

"It's almost been an overdrive of fear but also needing to advocate and be loud for my daughter. It doesn't go away, even now with her teachers. I have to remind myself that it's not the same as her being in the NICU and that it's just her Individual Education Plan (IEP), so relax; but it's hard. I lived with fear for her for years; no one came near her; nobody came to my house. I mean, it's a whole sad story of me not being able to move that feeling of being afraid for her. I was so much better, and then COVID came, and it threw me right back into my "nobody can come near my daughter" phase. She's not going out, not going to camp, or any of my other kids couldn't socialize with their friends, etc."

On the other hand, if you have clarity about what fear looks like for you, as well as specific instances in which you addressed your fears head on, you are one step ahead of the game. In my coaching practice, I typically encourage my clients, at a minimum, to answer the first question above (i.e. What does fear or being fearful look and/or feel like for you?) because it taps into their awareness, which is the first step towards processing in a healthy way. Processing can look differently depending on you and your situation. Some examples are:

- Requesting small bits of information at a time (**Reason:** Gives you control and autonomy; prevents overwhelm, which can trigger fear.)
- Identifying one thing or person that helps you feel less afraid (**Reason:** Creates your built-in support system.)
- Journaling about your fear (**Reason**: Writing it down makes it less scary and can help you produce your own solutions.)
- Using a past experience of you being fearless as a pattern for your present situation (**Reason**: Tapping into your own internal resources and strengths.)
- Saying you are afraid **(Reason:** Calling your fear aloud minimizes its strength over you.)

Be curious with yourself as you explore fear. This may sound like an odd thing to say, but, in my professional experience, I've found that oftentimes, we haven't taken the time to dig deeper into the who, what, and how of our feelings or the reasons we're feeling them. What beliefs we have about that emotion and our response to it. Where does that learned response come from, etc.

We will look at some of these concepts further in the Action section below.

Given that you are walking through this Fear section with me, it is telling me that fear may be stopping you from moving forward. Hence, I encourage you to start asking yourself some of the questions above. Be honest and gentle with yourself as you pull back the layers of fear that exist for you in your life. Be open to exploring and addressing fear so that you begin to shift, navigate, and own this emotion, so you live your life in a less fearful and more confident manner.

ACTION

One NICU parent I interviewed talked about the importance of identifying what you are feeling as a way of moving forward. I discuss this same strategy in the grief section of this book, and it is also a part of the processing piece about fear in the Exploration section.

The international author and Psychologist, the late Susan Jeffers, PhD, wrote a book back in the 1980's called *Feel the Fear and Do It Anyway*. In a nutshell, it is about facing your fears, and its message is still relevant today. The title sums this up, as it's not about ignoring or denying the fear inside of you but about addressing it head on so that you move from a place of pain to one of healing.

When our son was diagnosed with the eye disease ROP and we were told he was blind, shivers ran down my spine. I was scared for him, for us as his parents, and for what the future held or didn't hold for all of us. Despite my fear, shortly after his diagnosis, I reached out to all the specialist physicians and organizations for his condition around the world I could find. I spent days and weeks googling them, researching their work, and calling or emailing them. I honestly did not know what their response would be or even if they would respond, but I knew that I had to act and gather as much information as possible. Knowing that I was doing something despite my fear helped to minimize it because each time I contacted a specialist, my confidence grew a bit more.

Dr. Jeffers shared a multitude of strategies in the book, but one of my favorites, which I've adapted and use often in my coaching practice, is called the No-Lose Model. The premise of this model is that when you are trying to move forward in a situation, you can become so worried and fearful about making the wrong decision that you make no decision at all and remain stuck. Her model encourages you to look at not what will go wrong but what will go right regardless of what decision you make or the path you choose. She calls the outcomes and opportunities of any decision made "goodies" and encourages the reader to find them.

Likewise, when you are dealing with fear, as you and many parents I've worked with are, it is an emotion that can become so consuming that it causes you to either do nothing and worry or do something and worry. You may find yourself stuck with fear of making the wrong decision for your child, for your family, or for yourself, but it's important to acknowledge when you become unstuck, as the following story shows:

A NICU mother from the USA who had two pre-term birth experiences at 24-weeks and 34-weeks, respectively, shared how she dealt with and healed from the fear and trauma of these experiences. During our conversation, I noticed that she had naturally used the concepts of this No-Lose model as part of her healing when she made a big professional decision that was connected to her personal experience. She decided to step down from leading the non-profit organization she'd founded to help other NICU parents and shared:

"On a day-to-day basis, emotional health-wise, I'm working on my transition plan, having turned the darkest, worst experience into something positive. I used to feel like if I stopped now, then all the work I had done would've been for nothing. Now I say, 'No you've helped so many people that if it stops now, I'll be sad as there are still so many families out there to help.' But for me personally, I no longer feel that I have to be the savior and carry it all."

In her decision, the "goodies" she found along the way were: 1) It's ok to say "enough," and 2) Stopping would not invalidate her work or self-worth.

I've adapted the title of Dr. Jeffers' model slightly from a No-Lose to a Win-Win. For my clients and for you, I want to remove the word lose, to prevent that word from feeding into your subconsciousness because it has a negative connotation to it. To help you better navigate and manage your fear, I invite you to consider facing this emotion via the following questions:

- How is Fear showing up for you now?
- What are the "goodies" if you face your fears?
- What are the "goodies" if you don't?

The idea is a simple yet powerful one in that any decision you make has positive things within it, even if you are not seeing or feeling the benefits of it now. Many parents I interviewed shared how, when the worst of their fears happened (e.g., being in the NICU, having a child die, having a child with special needs), the hardest part was trying to find some good or purpose or sense in it all.

It can be difficult and conflicting to search for a sense of purpose after having a traumatic experience. An American Bereaved mother of twins described it in this way:

"Finding an online preemie and bereaved parent support group community was a 'lifesaver' for me, but do I wish I'd never met them? Of course, because that would mean that my sons would be here. In trying to find a meaning behind that loss, maybe my sons felt I needed more people in my life to connect with. It's because of my sons that I have all these people in my life, who I wouldn't have had otherwise."

Journaling:

Get your notebook or piece of paper and write down your answers to the following questions:

1. How does Fear show up for you?
2. What do you want to change about Fear in your life?
3. How will you know when you've achieved it? (i.e. What will you be doing, saying, thinking, or feeling differently than now).

Write down any other thoughts that are coming up for you about Fear.

GRIEF

*Grief: A deep and poignant multifaceted response
to loss, bereavement, or suffering*

Over half (55%) of the parents I interviewed identified grief as a common emotion they experienced, which I feel highlights the pervasiveness of it.

Grief is a loss response. We tend to think of grief as being one dimensional by manifesting itself in death or bereavement, but as the definition above suggests, this is not the only aspect of grief. We will delve into these other aspects shortly, but I invite you to sit down with me for a moment on this path of bereavement.

Death is a natural part of life, but the death of a child feels so unnatural because it is. It's so out of the norm, that we don't even have a name for it. This is highlighted by a saying I heard years ago, which is:

A wife who loses a husband is called a widow.

A husband who loses a wife is called a widower.

A child who loses his parents is called an orphan.

There is no word for a parent who loses a child.

That's how awful the loss is.

What word is even adequate to describe the pain that is indescribable when loss occurs? When interviewing bereaved parents for this book, it became apparent that there was not one word that existed because there were too many elements of grief present. This made it difficult to name them all. This is why I prefer the part of grief's definition which mentions its multifaceted aspect. We'll spend time walking through some of the many elements of grief through the stories of some of the bereaved parents I interviewed. They used a range of words, phrases, or narratives in an attempt to describe the crushing pain they felt.

An Australian NICU, Bereaved, and Special Needs mother who lost several babies during the second trimester, including her 25-week preterm twin who died, shared that she had *"lost five heartbeats"* as a way of capturing her profound loss experiences. She further described the surrealness of her grief, which showed up at her infant son's funeral in this way:

"I don't know how I got through that. I remember telling a friend, 'My legs are moving; my heart's beating; I'm breathing, but I'm not here.' That part of the brain protects you or something because I remember bits and pieces but not a huge amount."

This is what I call being present but not present, in which you are there physically but not mentally or emotionally. I see this occurring frequently with clients in my coaching practice who are going through any type of trauma.

Grief also has an incredulous element to it in that people cannot quite believe that what has happened to them has. One NICU and Bereaved mother of 25-week triplets from the USA expressed this aspect of grief when describing her thoughts after one of her triplets died at 14 months old after being re-hospitalized.

"I was prepared for another emergency room visit and that we would go to the Pediatric Intensive Care Unit (PICU), then go to the respiratory floor and stay there for a week. That is what I thought was going to happen. When we left the NICU 14 months earlier, I thought we'd left the worst behind us. It never even crossed my mind that she could die after we got home."

Parents also talked about the permanence of grief. Death happens, and there is nothing you can do to change it. This was expressed in the words of a NICU and Bereaved mother from Germany who had 25-week preterm twins and lost one of the twins shortly after birth.

"Our biggest trauma was that we lost our daughter. It is really important for us that people understand that when you lose a twin, a triplet, or a quadruplet, when you lose one of them, this will be forever. You will not have them in the end. That one child, and this influences you, your decisions, your whole life forever."

Sometimes grief feels like it is playing a cruel trick on you that no one finds funny. This is how a Bereaved mother from the USA of a 29-weeker who was born stillborn described it:

"I was in the hospital on bedrest trying to get far enough along so he wasn't born too premature because I have a kidney disease. I was 29 weeks. During routine vitals, there was no heartbeat. I had a C-section that night. It was a cord accident. The cord had wrapped around his head, body, and left leg. I couldn't believe that we'd fought this hard to get me far enough along and he dies of a cord accident."

As I have frequently mentioned throughout our walk together in this book, the common emotions we're exploring are not linear, and each of them can be felt separately or simultaneously. Several bereaved parents of multiples I interviewed talked of being fearful of losing their other child or children. When one of her 23-week twins died shortly after birth, this NICU and Bereaved mother from the USA shared how she was in such constant fear of losing her surviving son that she delayed the funeral of her son, who was deceased. She shared:

"We were told so many times that they didn't know if he was going to make it. The initial thought for me when the funeral home had to come to the hospital to meet us was, 'I don't want to bury my son who had passed because if anything happened to my surviving son, I wanted them to be buried together.' It was so heavy on me that we did not have my son's funeral for almost five weeks. For so long, I was always kind of expecting my surviving son to not make it."

Despite the heaviness of grief, it can also provoke kindness in others which was shown to one bereaved mother of 22-week twins just after they had died soon after their birth. She shared:

"I honestly can't remember if they kept them in the room after they'd both passed. It's just a blur. I remember my mom and brother staying overnight in the room with me, and I remember a nurse bringing both of my boys in to get them washed. Treating them carefully, dressing them, and giving me as much time as I needed with them. The nurse treated them like they were living babies, and for that I will be forever appreciative of."

This reminds me that when you least expect it, light can always pierce through the darkness.

There were many other bereaved parents I interviewed who shared their experiences of grief for their lost children, but due to limited space, I'm not able to include them here. Hence, I want to take a moment to pause and honor them now.

Per the definition above, grief is about loss, but it is also important to understand that loss is not solely about death or bereavement. There are many reasons why people may feel grief in the absence of bereavement. Some of these include, but are not limited to:

- *Living grief*: Parents described this as grieving their child even though that child is alive. They also expressed shame at even having this type of grief. An American NICU, Bereaved, and Special Needs mother whose child has complex special needs, explained her grief in this way:

  "I have a survivor who shouldn't have survived but did, and he has so many hardships in his life. There is a lot of grieving because I'm grieving someone that is living and sitting next to me."

- *Grief of pregnancy*: This is grieving not having a normal pregnancy, labor, and delivery. A common experience for parents who could not complete their pregnancy and/or had a pre-term birth. One NICU mother from the USA of a 24-week preterm infant shared a raw and graphic description of this type of grief in the following way:

  "I have very vivid memories of me crying and sobbing at night alone. The nurse came and was trying to understand what was causing it. I said I just miss my baby. She said, "I can take you to see him.". This was a

very profound moment because I said, 'No, I miss him in me.' It felt like a rape. I had a lot of guilt of even saying that word, but I felt like I'd been raped of my baby. I didn't labor, didn't push him. I was put to sleep, and they took him out, and I woke up."

- ***Parenting grief*:** This is grieving what you thought and/or expected your entry into parenthood would look like or what your parenting journey was going to be. This showed up with a lot of the parents I interviewed, but particularly with parents of children with Special Needs. An American NICU and Special Needs father of a 24-week preterm infant expressed it like this:

    "I struggle because of our child's special needs. It limits our options, both professional and life options. We have to think about things differently than the normal parent and make decisions in a different way. I have no resentment of our child, but it has changed our lives. It's life-limiting in a way or maybe life-altering is a better word, but this has to be put into context with the love we have for our child and the joy he brings to us.".

There are countless more grief stories, situations, and experiences parents shared with me. The list is endless and unique to each individual parent because grief is personal. No one can or should tell you how you should experience it. Despite this very personal aspect of grief, research shows that there are three main types of grief that are felt:

- Anticipatory: When you anticipate or expect a loss (e.g., terminal illness)

- Normal: The normal or expected feelings and behaviors of sadness after a loss, and
- Complicated: This can involve different types of grief, inclusive of:
  - Delayed: Your reaction to loss is postponed until later, sometimes years later
  - Chronic: Your grief is prolonged, persistent, or long-lasting
  - Exaggerated: Your reaction to loss is intense, extreme, or excessive above the normal grief response, and
  - Masked: When you try to suppress your grief and not deal with it.

The grief experienced by the majority of the parents I interviewed fell into the complicated grief category and included any of the four aspects of this grief. When I experienced my multiple pregnancy losses, especially the second trimester ones, I felt uncomfortable even admitting to myself or anyone else that they happened, let alone sharing how emotionally painful they were. Hence, I masked and delayed my grief, and only started to speak about it more in the past few years. Even though I have, I still find myself being cautious in how I share my grief and with whom.

It is also important to remember that parents who lose a child may be at different points along their grief journey and respond to or manifest their grief in completely different ways. An Australian NICU and Bereaved mother of 27-week and 30-week preterm infants, in which the latter died at 7 years old due to another medical condition, shared her difficulties of being at different grieving points with her husband in this way:

"It's frustrating because we're at different phases and the conversations are different. He feels that I'm letting go

where he's still holding on. It's a totally different emotion. I still remember her but in a different way because I'm able to grieve and let out the grief, thanks to therapy, whereas he is still retaining the grief. It's the conversation we're continually having because we're at different stages of this emotion.

Grief can also have an adverse impact based on the response of others. One Bereaved parent from the USA who experienced multiple pregnancy losses put it this way:

"Loss is a funny thing. You're not supposed to have it happen. My mom asked me after my first loss, 'What are you learning from this experience?' I said, I'm learning that people are dumb and ask really stupid questions."

This mother had experienced so many inappropriate and hurtful responses from well-meaning people that she became frustrated and sarcastic.

Grief can be death, but as we've seen, it can also mean a lot of other things connected to someone experiencing a deep loss. A loss that is not a one-size-fits-all kind of feeling or response but individual to them. Grief has many levels, depths, and manifestations and affects us emotionally, spiritually, physically, socially, financially, and every other way in between.

Like all the emotions we are discussing, they can easily cause us to feel stuck, preventing us from taking the necessary steps to move forward in our lives. Grief is no exception, and because this emotion is all about the loss of something or someone that you won't get back, there is a finality to it that makes it more difficult to accept or manage.

A French NICU and Bereaved mother of preterm infant twins, in which one died in utero at 21 weeks and the surviving twin was born at 27 weeks, while they resided in another country, described the finality of grief in this way:

"The most difficult part was the loss of my daughter because I had lost my brother when I was eight years old and he was 12. So, I had that dream that my little daughter would be buried with my brother in France. It was impossible because you couldn't legally bring a dead baby to France. You had to do cremation to be able to do so, and cremation wasn't in my mind at all. So, my poor little girl was in the morgue for months, and months, and months, and the NICU kept calling me, saying that I must make a decision because they couldn't keep her forever. That was heartbreaking because I didn't want to do cremation, but in the end, that was the only way for me to take her to France. It was very hard for me to make that decision."

In this mother's case, she knew whatever decision she made about her child would be irreversible.

Your grief may have encompassed one or all the types of grief mentioned in this section. It may also very likely include other types of grief that are not listed above.

Grief is silent but loud.

Silence can make the grief experience feel real yet obscure, tangible yet surreal, felt yet not understood, worthy yet shameful, and light yet heavy. This silence can prevent or slow down any forward-moving action with this emotion.

This silence can come from a myriad of sources. The person experiencing grief. The people around the person experiencing grief. The societal and cultural mores and pressures about grief.

For example, in some societies, there can be an uncomfortableness surrounding grief. An American Bereaved mother of 27-week preterm twins in which one survived and the other did not put it this way when sharing her experience of feeling the need to try and comfort others while going through her own grief:

"In a grief situation, I've found that you often spend a lot of time making other people feel better about your pain versus taking care of yourself."

Sometimes with grief, the ramifications or consequences of it are thrust upon us too quickly, way before we're ready for them. A Brazilian NICU mother of 26-week preterm infants in which one survived but the other didn't, described one unexpected consequence of her grief in this way:

"One of my sons was born stillborn and stayed with me in my room. The nurse was amazing and said, 'Let's take pictures.' I thought to myself, 'with a dead baby?' It was so weird because it had never crossed my mind. To have pictures of a dead baby."

Nothing in her initial idea of birth, delivery, or parenting would or could have prepared her for that. I've yet to read or hear of a pregnancy book that informs the reader, "Oh, by the way, one of your babies will be born dead, and afterwards you will take pictures of your baby's body." I don't know anyone who will say, "Yes, sign me up for that." I'm not trying to be facetious, but if you think that this actually happened and happens, for me, this again speaks to the abnormality and surrealness that exists within the NICU, Bereaved, and Special Needs worlds.

Sometimes this surrealness combined with the sheer heaviness of this emotion may cause parents to not even have words to articulate their grief. Hence, they are silent. This silence can sometimes be misunderstood. The NICU and Bereaved mother from France I mentioned earlier, shared her experience with this:

"My daughter passed at 21 weeks in utero. This was why my son was born prematurely because I got an infection from the fact that she was still there. Then my son got an infection, and they couldn't treat it with an antibiotic and said it would be more effective treating him with an antibiotic outside my womb than inside. So, we had to deliver both of them for the sake of my son. The most difficult part was the loss of my daughter. I started therapy to deal with this. I'm not a talker at all, so the first time I started my therapy, the therapist bluntly told me, 'I'm wasting my time with you because you have nothing to say.' I tried again, but I could never go really deep in talking of my grief. I think I never had a chance to grieve."

Hmmm, I won't say here what my thoughts are on the therapist's comment, but I do think that perhaps I'm going to have to write another book for professionals entitled *What Not to Say*, or better yet, *Know When to Shut Up*. One takeaway from this mother's experience is realizing that grief can be loud, but it can also be silent. Both are equally valid. Several parents I interviewed talked about this silent element of grief and how it is connected to the feeling of shame which we mentioned earlier.

Let's pause for a moment to briefly touch on shame as it relates to grief. Shame, as discussed in both the trauma section and earlier in this grief section, is a distressed feeling from thinking you've done something wrong. Grief can be a significant contributor and exacerbator of shame, especially when you don't feel worthy enough to grieve or feel that you're even allowed to. This can happen with living grief we mentioned earlier, but it can also happen with pregnancy loss. In either situation, parents shared that they did not feel like their loss experience mattered as much or was viewed as being worthy to others in comparison to a parent who had experienced a stillbirth or the death of a baby or child who had lived outside the womb. One Bereaved mother from the USA who'd had several pregnancy losses shared her experience after losing her first one:

"Other people didn't acknowledge my child. This was the first time I thought to myself, 'Oh, maybe losing my baby the way I lost my baby means that I didn't really have a baby."

In a way, although most likely unintentional, this feels like a form of gaslighting, in which someone unintentionally tries to discount, minimize, or deny your reality in such a way as to make you doubt yourself or be confused by your own reality.

I remember having similar feelings of doubt, some self-inflicted, some inflicted by others, during my own pregnancy losses and wondering if they constituted a *real* baby by society's standards. The first trimester, second trimester, my son's twin? Were they real? Did they exist? These were the types of questions swirling around in my head. There were times that I even tried to determine which loss was significant enough so that people would understand why I felt so sad. Which one could somehow justify my tears? Justify my grief? For me, all of them. I have a treasure box in my bedroom where I've kept tucked away every single ultrasound of all four of my children who I didn't get to hug. I take them out and stare at them sometimes to remember hearing the sound of each of their heartbeats and remind myself that, yes, they existed. They were loved even if not held.

This questioning of whether your experience is worth grieving about can manifest itself in various forms with parents, namely:

- NICU parents who may have had a shorter or what may be deemed a less complicated stay, or with NICU parents whose children are not born prematurely.
- Pregnancy versus infant loss, as we've just mentioned, and
- Special Needs parents of children with mild, moderate, or severe special needs, trying to determine which families' situation is better or worse.

While I can understand our innate human need to compare or figure out who or what is more worthy, I ask that you take caution in doing this because it is a slippery slope. When we do this, our perspective becomes skewed because we start judging others' experiences through our own lens. This is rarely beneficial for you or your healing because—your lens won't ever fit their lives, nor will their lens fit yours.

This is not to minimize or downplay in any way the horrific grief experienced from a baby's death, an extremely lengthy stay in the NICU, or a complex and/or chronic special needs diagnosis, but just a gentle reminder that everyone's lived experience with grief is their own. There should not be a race or competition to determine whose grief is worse, more profound, more worthy of being manifested or understood.

The last aspect of grief I want to mention is related to time. Grief does not care about time. By this I mean it can and often does hit you whenever it wants. At the exact moment of your loss, many years later, or which often happens, at multiple points along your life's journey. A saying I've heard often that, although spoken with good intention, is not helpful with grief is, "Time will heal all wounds." From personal experience, it doesn't, and several parents I interviewed said a similar thing. Time can give you needed space and distance, though, to start learning how to live with your grief in a way that is more beneficial, healthier, and even more joyful.

This reminds me of the words the United Kingdom's Queen Elizabeth II wrote as part of her condolence message after the September 11th, 2001, terrorist attacks, in which she said, "Grief is the price we pay for love." Her words were adapted from an original passage in the book entitled *Bereavement: Studies of Grief in Adult Life*, by psychiatrist Dr. Colin Murray Parkes. In it, he wrote, "The pain of grief is just as much part of life as the joy of love. It is perhaps the price we pay for love, the cost of commitment. To ignore this fact or to pretend that it is not so, is to put on emotional blinkers which leave us unprepared for the losses that will inevitably occur in our own lives and unprepared to help others cope with losses in theirs."

I guess Dr. Parkes words can be seen as an integral part of navigating not just through grief but all the emotions we're discussing in this book. We can't ignore them or pretend they don't exist or don't really affect us. It's perfectly ok to acknowledge that they do and use them to not only help yourself but also help others. In other words, remove your "emotional blinkers."

So, let's start doing that with your grief. Remove your blinkers and remove or at least mitigate the silence, unworthiness, and shame from grief that's preventing you from healing and moving forward.

REFLECTION

Given that grief is such a common emotion felt as noted by the parents I interviewed, there is an importance of managing it in a way that it doesn't consume you. We will begin the process of reflecting on your grief in a manner similar to how we have reflected on the other emotions—by being curious. In thinking about grief in general, and most importantly, your own grief, I invite you to consider the following questions:

- What insight do you want from your grief?
- How will you know that you have gotten this grief insight?
- How will you use this insight to move you forward?

You will note that these questions are focused on gaining insight, which is defined as having a deeper and more accurate understanding of something. Hence, they are designed to gently push you towards getting a more authentic take on your grief, knowing where you are with this emotion and where you want to be.

EXPLORATION

In my coaching practice, I often provide a good chunk of space and time for my clients to sit with questions like the above. Having some degree of clarity as you navigate any challenge assists you in identifying what change is essential and what isn't. It also frees you up to dance around and be curious about how you want that change to look. To explore further, I invite you to consider these questions:

- What change is essential in my grief?
- What change is not essential in my grief?
- What do I want my grief to look like?

Due to your lived experience as a Bereaved, NICU, or Special Needs parent, grief won't leave you. Most parents I've worked with are not trying to remove it from their lives as it is an integral part of their identity. Rather they want to have a healthier perspective of a relationship with grief. Let's consider ways of doing this.

ACTION
Grief-Naming Exercise

- Think of and write down at least three (3) grief situations that you're experiencing/have experienced (e.g., loss of child, birth experience, idea of parenting, etc.).
- Look over your list and select the one grief situation that is causing or has caused you the most pain.
- Highlight or mark it on your piece of paper.

Now Pause, take a deep breath, and slowly count to five to re-center and

- Look back at your chosen grief situation. Sit with it for a moment and read or re-read it aloud to yourself.
- With it in mind, answer or at least reflect on the following three (3) questions:
  - How does it feel to name your specific griefs?
  - What do your named griefs tell you about yourself, if anything?
  - Which of your three named griefs do you most want to change your feelings about?

This "change" I mention is not about you altering what you've experienced or are experiencing in your grief; nothing can or should change that, but rather it is about adjusting or tweaking your approach towards it in a more empowering and compassionate way. Empowering so that you are stronger to navigate it and compassionate so that you are gentle with yourself through the navigation. That's it. Sit with your answers and let them be with you for a while. Try to avoid overanalyzing them; just let them be.

As we saw in the Fear section, research has shown that when you name your fear, it becomes less scary and has less power over you. I believe it's the same with naming your grief. When our son was born at 24 weeks and we'd lost his twin in utero a few weeks earlier, I cried a lot, yes, but I'm not sure if I really allowed myself to grieve. I surely didn't spend time naming my grief, but now in hindsight, I think it would have helped me if I had. I would have said that I was grieving an incomplete pregnancy, my body failing me, my angel baby, a normal life as a mom, what could have been, etc. I wish I'd been cognizant enough to do that, but I wasn't.

To continue to process your grief, I invite you to consider these additional exploratory questions as you move forward:

- Where are you now in your grief story?
- What is grabbing your heart about your grief?
- What is this telling you?
- Where do you want to be in your grief story?
- Name one thing you will do to get you closer to what you want.

Your responses to the last question will provide you with a personal blueprint or road map for better navigating and owning your grief and its impact in your life.

Journaling:

Grab a notebook or piece of paper and write down your answers to the following questions:

1. How does Grief show up for you?
2. What do you want to change about Grief in your life?
3. How will you know when you've achieved it? (i.e. What will you be doing, saying, thinking, or feeling differently than now).

Write down any other thoughts that are coming up for you about Grief.

— EMOTION —

GUILT

Guilt: When a person feels that they have violated some sort of moral code or standard and are responsible for it.

"Guilt. I had lots of guilt for multiple things. What did or didn't I do that got us in this situation? Having to leave them every day to go home because I had a two-year-old at home at the time who I'd never left. It felt like my heart was in two places, and I felt so torn about where I wanted to be and could be. Twenty-two years down the road, guilt is still the emotion that resonates the most. Forgiving myself yet there's nothing to forgive. I just struggled with this for so long, and it was all self-imposed."

(An American NICU mother to 25-week preterm twins)

In general, people can feel guilty at different points in their lives, but the guilt of NICU, Bereaved, or Special Needs parents appears to take on a personality of its own. A large majority, 61%, of the parents I interviewed, expressed feelings of guilt or identified it as the primary emotion they struggle with. Wow. This beast of an emotion rears its ugly head so often and in so many ways in our lives, but we rarely talk about it, out loud at least, for many reasons.

Although there are several studies in literature on guilt types or categories, there doesn't seem to be a universally accepted classification of guilt. Saying this, I did come across literature that highlighted the work of Mathias Hirsch, a German psychiatrist, psychoanalyst, and author, who classified this emotion in a way that seems easy to understand and made sense, at least to me. He highlighted the following four (4) categories of guilt, from a child development point of view:

- **Basic:** Feeling of not being wanted (e.g., child not being wanted by parents, etc.)
- **Vitality:** Guilt from having big desires to surpass or be better than others (e.g., being the better child, etc.)
- **Separation:** Desire for autonomy (e.g., wanting to be separate from parents; own identity)
- **Trauma-related:** Extreme conflict (e.g., severe cases of abuse-violence)

One aspect of his classification as it potentially relates to you is the notion of trauma-related guilt. This is what the majority of parents I interviewed and have worked with in my coaching practice experience. If you flip to our section on Trauma, this type of guilt is similar to complex trauma. Several traumatic things are happening simultaneously, and this is a common experience voiced by NICU, Bereaved, and Special Needs parents.

Most parents I spoke with felt ashamed for feeling guilty. There's that shame word again, but the reality of it is that we *do* feel guilty. Many of my clients, and me too, and probably you as well, have felt this emotion deeply and frequently but have become experts at covering it. We fool ourselves into thinking that we never felt it or that we no longer feel it. In addition, we will jump through hoops to avoid even saying the word and are masters at coming up with other adjectives to attempt to describe how we feel. Adjectives such as uncomfortable, anxious, confused, sad, upset, etc.

Now I don't think we do this intentionally or to be dishonest with ourselves. Rather I believe that it is incredibly difficult for us to articulate and admit to this hugely conflicting feeling that we have. Conflicting because, on one hand, we feel happy that our child is alive but, on the other hand, guilty that they are in the NICU, or grateful that we experienced pregnancy but guilty that our baby died. Perhaps we feel thankful that our child can attend school but guilty that they have special needs which make their educational struggle harder. Guilt is crushing and can feel even more suffocating because it often shows up accompanied by its buddies, what I like to call its common bedfellows. These are anxiety, anger, and grief—several of the other emotions highlighted in this book. Sometimes it may feel like they are all dancing together, bent on causing havoc in your head and heart. Each of these emotions individually can be overwhelming, but when they all pile up in the emotional bandwagon together, especially when they are unresolved which they sometimes are, it can be soul-crushing.

Even more conflicting is that this "moral code" within guilt that we feel like we're breaking does not even need to be accurate. Accuracy has nothing to do with our emotions. I've had many NICU parents, especially those who had a premature birth, say to me, "It's my fault my baby came early" or "Something is wrong with me" or "I must've done something to cause this." These feelings and thoughts can persist even if there is absolutely no truth or evidence of them.

A NICU and Bereaved multiple-birth mother from the USA shared this about her internal guilt-shame conflict in this way:

"When they were delivered prematurely at 25 weeks, I felt this extreme guilt that I was being punished because of the selective reduction I'd done because they had started out as quintuplets. That was what I thought—that my children had to suffer because I made that decision. First, it was the fear that they wouldn't survive delivery, and then it was, 'They're suffering and it's my fault.' The shame and guilt from this thinking took many years to undo."

Sometimes guilt produces extra layers of emotions that further complicate and weigh down an already heavy feeling. I think of these extra layers as emotional detours in that they may take you the longer route to get to your destination or desired outcome. The reason I'm bringing it up here in this space is for you to be able to recognize them when they arise, so you don't get off track with the healing process for your primary emotion of guilt. During my interviews with parents, one emotional detour raised was shame. We discussed this in the section on grief, but as we're seeing here, it can also feature prominently in guilt as well. It can make you self-conscious and negatively evaluate yourself.

One NICU mother of a 25-week preterm infant from the USA described shame in this way

"If nobody says to you that it's not your fault, all you have left is that internal blame. That narrative of what did I do wrong."

You can see from this mother's experience how her negative self-evaluation (i.e., "I'm a failure") stemmed from shame tied into her guilt (i.e., "I'm to blame").

Guilt can be felt by all, including fathers. This group of parents (i.e., fathers) feel guilty for not being able to "fix" the situation. At the risk of sounding like I'm simply overgeneralizing, men more often than women, can sometimes be hard-wired to fix stuff. This isn't everyone, of course, but it happens. When fathers realize they can't "fix" their child, they can feel less of a person, a provider, just less of everything.

A NICU and Special Needs father from the USA shared:

"I think to overcompensate for the trauma I was feeling but couldn't explain, I overindulged and worked long hours. I felt that I could control my work, but not what was happening to my child in the NICU."

For mothers in particular, the moral code we feel has been violated is our bodies, as seen in one of the mother's comments previously. We feel like our bodies have violated the code of being able to have a healthy and complication-free pregnancy and delivery and that we're 100% responsible for this violation. Preemie moms often feel they have failed at protecting their children by not being able to keep them inside for the duration of their pregnancy. They can feel angry at their bodies for not working properly. Special needs parents can feel they've failed at having a "normal" child, and I use the word "normal" very loosely and am intentionally putting it in quotation marks because what IS normal anyway?

I experienced these emotions myself, both as the mother of a 24-weeker and mother of a child who was now blind. Of course, I didn't say, "Gigi, you have broken the sacred code of motherhood" by failing to be a normal one, but somewhere in my subconscious, a version of it was firmly embedded into my psyche. This feeling of failure and guilt was further compounded by, as mentioned in the Preface, a doctor's scribble in the medical record notes I received months after we'd left the NICU. The doctor's entry described me as a "woman having incomplete pregnancies." He could have just as easily written a "woman who failed motherhood" because that is exactly how I felt reading those words.

Why did one of the few things that was legible in my medical records have to be this descriptive yet hurtful comment about me, my womanhood … my failures? My mind instantly whipped itself into a frenzy as I told myself, "See, I told you, you were a failure—you couldn't even complete a normal pregnancy like everyone else. Even the doctor knows this and has officially labeled you as 'incomplete.'" Intellectually, I know now that my thinking then was a load of rubbish, but in that moment, it wasn't. It was true, and I was drawn into all the junk—hook, line, and sinker—and listened to and believed every single word I read and was telling myself.

Interestingly, I never read (that I can remember) or told myself that, independent of my supposed failures, I was strong and resilient. Which in hindsight, I was, given that all the while I was praying for and willing my son to live during our nearly six months in the NICU, I was also still grieving, albeit silently. Grieving for his twin we lost in utero as well as his sibling we'd lost the year before. I'm getting teary-eyed just thinking about it now, but that's the power of what buying and feeding into guilt and any of the emotions we're exploring can do to us—to you. It can give us a distorted and partial image of ourselves that feels so incredibly real and absolute that we hang onto it as our only truth. We never see, feel, or believe the other parts of our emotional selves. Especially the good parts.

It reminds me of when we read reviews for a product or event. There can be 100 comments in total with 99 people saying the product was absolutely fantastic and one person saying it was beyond awful. What do our eyes zero in on, and what do we believe? Yep, you guessed it—that one negative review. The impact of this can cause a behavior change because, even though we desperately need that product or want to attend that event, we don't. Likewise, the impact of the narrative we feed ourselves about guilt can also change our behavior by stopping us in our tracks, preventing us from moving forward. This can be compounded when our internal guilt is intertwined with our parental guilt, as one NICU mother from the USA of a 28-week preterm infant shared:

"As a parent, the guilt of not being there—of feeling like I abandoned my baby in their most vulnerable moments—stays with you. Even when you know the care they're receiving is saving their life, the ache of not being able to comfort them is immeasurable."

Remembering again that none of the emotions we're exploring in this book are linear, another American NICU mother of a 38-week full-term infant shared how guilt and fear danced together in her mind during her pregnancy in this way:

"When we decided to have another child, in the back of my head, I felt like a 3rd child was somewhat of a bonus baby, in some ways, whether it was right or wrong. I felt like I was somewhat overreaching because God had given me two healthy children. At week 11, there was a virus at my daughter's school that could get into the uterus of the mother and cause complications with that pregnancy. So, I was petrified and thought, 'Look at that, exactly what you put out there is happening,' Then they were testing me for that virus, and initially I didn't have it, but then quickly thereafter, I got it and was diagnosed with a medical condition and pregnancy complication. Again, in my head, I was thinking, 'This is my 3rd child, and maybe I shouldn't have tried for this pregnancy.'"

REFLECTION

Let's pause for a moment and anchor ourselves before we delve further into guilt awareness.

I invite you to reflect on and answer these two questions, either in your journaling space, your notebook, or rhetorically in your head.

- What do I feel guilty about as a parent?
- Where does my guilt come from?

Jot down the first things that come to your mind. Be honest with yourself without judgment. The pages of this book are a judgment free space, so give yourself permission to be truthful to you. You're allowed, and it makes you much more aware of yourself. Both questions above are important, but if you can spend a bit of time on the second one, please do. Uncovering the source of your guilt is an important step towards healing because it helps you to increase your awareness and recognition of your triggers for guilt. These may be different, depending on the context, environment, and people you're around. Bereaved parents have shared feelings of both guilt and grief if they see a child who is the same age as their child would've been had they lived. This is a different context than for special needs parents who may feel guilty about the hardships their child has to face.

As you reflect on the questions above, be mindful of your values, beliefs, and self-limiting beliefs about guilt. What do I mean by this?

Values are what you think or feel are important or worthwhile in life that informs your behavior and/or standards (e.g., loyalty, kindness, morality, family, sacrifice, authenticity, etc.). For example, a person who values honesty will always aim to be truthful to themselves and others.

Beliefs are accepting something is true or exists, especially without proof (e.g., Life is not fair, Spirituality is good, All governments are bad, All wealthy people are selfish, etc.).

A Self-Limiting Belief is any belief that stops you from moving forward (e.g., I'm not good enough, I can't, nobody will believe me, etc.). Hence, I am not qualified for that job, so I won't apply.

Within the context of guilt, this means:

- The importance you place on guilt is your values.
- What you accept about guilt are your beliefs.
- Anything that allows guilt to stop you in your tracks are your self-limiting beliefs.

I invite you to pause and sit with your responses to the reflective questions above. What do they tell you about yourself, the role guilt plays or has played in your life, the origin of this emotion for you?

Being self-aware, which is our ability to pay attention to and objectively evaluate ourselves, helps to lead us to a healthier space. Hence, whatever your answers were to the above increases your awareness in terms of guilt and its influence and impact on your life.

Additional ways to increase your awareness are:

- Journaling. Keep a daily journal and jot down every time you feel guilt. It doesn't have to be a long dissertation but a few words in bullet-form. To push yourself even further, also jot down the situation in which you are feeling guilt. Were you triggered by a word, memory, action? The more detailed and specific you are, the stronger your self-awareness is, which will assist you in being better able to address it more effectively.

- Honest Feedback. Ask your friends. Get feedback from others about whether you express your guilt to them and how. Make sure you ask people who you trust, feel safe with, and are honest with you, even if that is only one person. This reflective process can give you additional information into how guilt is showing up in the spaces and people around you. If left unchecked, guilt can fester and seep out through the pores of your being.

EXPLORATION

The next step is to explore a bit further to understand the permeation and compartmentalization of guilt to not only deepen the awareness and implication of it in your life but also gently challenge you to face your guilt so you can better process it. A NICU and Special Needs mother from the USA of a 29-week preterm infant shared:

"Guilt is throughout until this day the #1 emotion I feel. [There are] tons of types of guilt that come with that. For example, with his NEC surgery, with everything that was going on with him, and he was septic a few times. They gave him a 1% chance of survival. So, we've said goodbye to him multiple times. That guilt carries on. Especially at NEC symposiums, which are the hardest because I have a survivor who shouldn't have survived but did. I feel guilty that he has so many hardships in life that I feel like I caused because I wanted to have a baby so bad. It didn't matter what that baby had to face. So, there's a lot of survival guilt."

Keep in mind that all our feelings give us something, either positively or negatively, whether we realize it or not. From the positive perspective, it can give you an explanation for your parenting style (e.g., I am more lenient with my child because of their early birth). The negative viewpoint may give you a reason for not moving forward (e.g., I can't be happy because my child died). Guilt can give you a compass for how you view, process, and navigate your world.

One American NICU and Bereaved mother of 25-week preterm triplets in which two survived and one died over one year later, shared how not processing her guilt affected her and her world:

"Well, I didn't for a long time; I just didn't. I went for my six-week follow-up for my ob-gyn and they [her children] were all still alive but still quite sick and small. [One daughter] in particular struggled for so long. She [my doctor] didn't even put me in an exam room because as soon as her assistant brought me back, I just started crying and [felt] it was just: this is my fault, I did this. So, she put me on Zoloft."

Another NICU mother of 27-week preterm infants from the USA described her complete avoidance and its impact in this way:

"Maybe there is a layer of plastic or acrylic, [and] all these emotions are behind the glass. Sometimes it feels like you didn't really experience these things, like this didn't happen to me. It happened to someone else. I think at some point I will remove the glass and work on it which I plan on doing ... Right now, and there is this avoidance piece where I say, 'I'm too busy to sit with my thoughts.'"

I invite you to consider these parents' stories and ask yourself whether you have processed your own guilt.

As you do, consider the two concepts of compartmentalization and processing that we've highlighted earlier. Several parents I interviewed compartmentalized their emotions, whether consciously or unconsciously like the parents above, which is understandable, particularly when you are in an acute traumatic space. Compartmentalizing can become your life jacket and life saver. This means that it temporarily keeps you afloat emotionally until you are ready and able to process your guilt.

To thrive, processing must occur. When my son was born, I remember everything that happened so distinctly, but I surely didn't process it then. I couldn't. Who could? In many ways, it felt like an "out-of-body" experience, similar to what one of the mothers shared above. It was just too surreal to comprehend, let alone process or deal with. In that moment, I was only able to be in it, physically and mentally. My emotional experience of and healing from it would come later in drips and drabs, with some of the drabs only beginning to flow as I started to write the pages of this book. One way I started to process my experience was to acknowledge that it happened. This gives your experience validity and you the permission and freedom to embrace it and heal from it. Sometimes as we go through the NICU, Bereaved, or Special Needs experiences, we don't say what's happening to or within us. To do so gives you back your power as a parent.

To navigate your guilt more healthily, I invite you to consider these two questions:

- Have you compartmentalized your guilt? If so, how?
- Have you processed your guilt? Again, if so, how?

ACTION

1. **Acknowledge It.** Part of the power of guilt is that it can fester and grow in silence. Like cancer, it can be hidden and kept inside for so long that by the time you realize (or rather honestly acknowledge) that it is there, it's taken over you emotionally. You may find guilt incredibly difficult to bear and that it is permeating throughout various aspects of your life. All-consuming. Keeping it to yourself gives it more power to consume; hence, I don't want you to do this.

2. **Desired Outcome:** What is your desired outcome for the guilt you feel? Sometimes we may know where we are, but we are not so sure about where we're going or want to go. This question starts you on that journey and promotes action to facilitate you getting there. As mentioned in the Anger section, in coaching, having an idea of your desired outcome/ end result is a part of evoking awareness and facilitating growth.

Journaling:

Get your notebook or piece of paper and write down your answers to the following questions:

1. How does Guilt show up for you?
2. What do you want to change about Guilt in your life?
3. How will you know when you've achieved it? (i.e. What will you be doing, saying, thinking, or feeling differently than now).

Next, write down any other thoughts that are coming up for you about Guilt.

STRESS/OVERWHELM

Stress: Having emotional strain or tension caused by adverse or demanding circumstances.

Overwhelm: To have a feeling of being completely engulfed and overcome with emotion.

Although two different words, parents I have worked with in the NICU, Bereavement, and Special Needs spaces often use them together and interchangeably. Hence, we will do the same here. Outside of these spaces, stress and overwhelm are sometimes the first words people experiencing trauma generally use when expressing how they feel. They can become who we are, how we function, how we speak, how we identify with ourselves. In other words, they become our state of being and our default response, showing up in every situation, even when we're not actually feeling them. For example, you're in the grocery store at the checkout, and the cashier asks, "How are you?" You immediately say "stressed," even if in that exact moment, you are not feeling stressed.

In the fast-paced and high-pressured society we live in nowadays, I sometimes wonder if we're "stressed by the stress" and "overwhelmed by the overwhelm." Meaning being continuously stressed and overwhelmed causes stress and overwhelm. It reminds me of a saying I first heard as a young adult: "I'm sick and tired of being sick and tired."

For the NICU, Bereaved, and Special Needs parents I interviewed, stress and overwhelm are not just simple default emotions or an off-handed response to life. Rather they are a genuine response to the trauma parents have experienced and a reality for their lives.

Although stress and overwhelm are emotions that often go hand-in-hand and are thought of and described together, there are some slight but important differences between the two that impact your healing. So, let us take a moment to review them separately before bringing them back together again.

There's a range of literature and information in existence about different types of stress, including but not limited to physical, psychological, emotional, etc. For the purpose of our time together, we won't explore every single one. Instead, we'll focus on the two most common ones, as these were the ones most frequently raised during my parent interviews and what I see in my coaching practice. According to The American Psychological Association (APA), there are two main types of stress. They are:

- **Acute:** Stress that occurs rapidly and unexpectedly, typically due to a new or recent event. It is the most common and usually short-term. An example of this type of stress would be getting caught in a traffic jam, having an argument with a loved one, running late, etc.

- **Chronic:** Stress that is ongoing over a long period of time. This is the most harmful and can lead to a range of mental and physical health problems (e.g., high blood pressure, diabetes, depression, anxiety, etc.).

The parents I interviewed experienced both types, with acute stress typically occurring during the initial parts of their journey (e.g., preterm birth, child loss, or receiving a special needs diagnosis).

Chronic stress showed up when faced with the daily challenges of bereavement, post-NICU, or the responsibility of caring for a medically fragile child or child with special needs.

Stress causes us to constantly worry and feel like something is going to happen that we won't be able to deal with. Similar to a cord that is constantly stretched to its limit, frays, and if not supported, eventually snaps.

I remember bringing our son home and feeling so worried and stressed out that he would stop breathing during the night or as soon as I closed my eyes, that I put his cot next to my side of the bed and every few minutes put my ear close to his mouth and nose to make sure I heard and felt his breath. I also stared at his chest while doing this to make sure I saw his chest rise and fall. My NICU parenting experience and subsequent circumstance of caring for a medically fragile baby only served to heighten my stress. This caused me to not only constantly feel tense but also anticipate and expect that something was going to happen.

Overwhelm is an all-consuming feeling and causes people to close in and shut down. That "I'm going to pull the covers over my head; I don't want to deal with it" kind of feeling. Some parents describe overwhelm as a drowning, sinking, or rollercoaster feeling, like everything is happening all at once; with too many moving parts, no pause button, and a feeling like the chaos can't be stopped.

It reminds me of a comment I heard the American comedian David Mann share when describing his depression. He said, "I felt like I was drowning, and the only way others would know I was drowning was if I drowned." I'm not equating overwhelm to depression, although for some people it may manifest in this way. Rather, I'm highlighting the similarities of this engulfing and all-consuming feeling they both can cause.

In some literature, overwhelm is described as stress overload by which people feel not or less capable of dealing with the physical and psychological stresses of life. Possible signs and symptoms of overwhelm from this perspective can include such things as:

- Health illnesses
- Anger and frustration
- Anxiety disorders
- Depression
- Eating disorders
- Sleeping disorders

This list is not exhaustive, but a quick glance at these symptoms shows you the overlap of emotions such as anger with stress/overwhelm and how one triggers or is a symptom of the other. This research highlighted the fact that anger could be a symptom of feeling overwhelmed, but from the anger section, we see that it is also a separate emotion in itself. Again, this highlights the non-linear and interconnecting aspects of all the emotions we experience.

The depth of the feeling of being overwhelmed was vividly described by an Irish NICU mother of a 25-week preterm infant as *"being eroded,"* which means to gradually be destroyed. This may sound like a strong word to use, but based on the parent interviews I conducted, it is an accurate description of the impact of this emotion on NICU, Bereaved, and Special Needs parents. This mother further explained that the stress and overwhelm began when her waters broke many weeks prior to her child's preterm birth, which led to her feeling emotionally depleted. She shared:

"For 12 weeks, I was being eroded, and by the time I got to the birth, I was a shadow of myself and had nothing left to give. No mental or physical reserves."

The ongoing stress of the situation this mother was in steadily built up to the point of her shutting down and zoning out. It was too much to carry. Stress builds up, overwhelm shuts down. This reminds me of a car. You can't drive it on empty. If you don't refuel it, you'll run out of gas and be stranded. Likewise, if you try to continue living in the traumatic parental space of overwhelm, you'll find yourself on empty, barely functioning, and will soon run out and zone out too. We must refuel our cars and refuel ourselves. Refueling and replenishing is a part of your healing.

To better understand and appreciate overwhelm and what's happening in our bodies when we feel it, Certified Trauma Professional Brad Hardie has a slightly different perspective for us to consider:

"We call it overwhelm for definition, but the body is actually doing exactly what it's supposed to. That's an interesting piece to the way we look at this. We label it as a traumatic experience, but in truth what the body's doing is because its one modus operandi is to keep the organism alive at all costs. That's what it is doing, but we fear that because we feel out of control, and it feels like it's doing something we're not used to. The body is doing what it's been designed to do for ages because, when a person experiences overwhelm or trauma, it moves into its primitive state and says, I need to either shut down, run, get out of this situation, pass out, whatever it is, and that's a primitive state for survival."

Hmmm, that feels refreshing to me and a little less scary. Knowing that overwhelm is a natural response to trauma will hopefully allow you to give yourself a little grace and space whenever these emotions creep up. Briefly going back to the car and gasoline analogy, overwhelm can be considered your indicator light to tell you something needs attention. As NICU, Bereaved, and Special Needs parents, what needs attention is you. Let's walk through how you can start doing that.

REFLECTION

Self-regulation is the ability to manage your behavior and reactions to your feelings and is an important strategy to combat stress and overwhelm. This is where we will begin our reflection.

I invite you to think of self-regulation as intentionally pausing for a specific amount of time. In the coaching world, this type of purposeful and controlled pause is recommended to be used before a person goes into a stressful situation, such as a difficult meeting at work. For stress and overwhelm, it can be used to help you mitigate or eliminate these emotions.

A structured way of implementing this is what I call the seven (7) second pause. When you feel the initial signs of stress and overwhelm in your body, such as tightening of your muscles, rapid breathing, chest pounding, sense of dread, etc., STOP and count to seven. Count in a slow, measured way like this: One……. Two……. Three……. Four……. etc.

In my coaching practice, when clients express feeling stress and overwhelm or if I sense either of these emotions being heightened, I note it and offer an invitation to breathe to self-regulate and re-center themselves. If they accept my invitation, it works 100% of the time. Feel free to use this simple but effective technique when needed.

To further reflect on the better managing of or healing from stress and overwhelm, let's uncover how they may be manifesting in your life and parenting journey now. Ask yourself the following questions to increase your awareness and move you forward:

- When do I feel the most stressed/overwhelmed?
- When do I feel the least stressed/overwhelmed?

It is important to know when you are experiencing stress and overwhelm, but also when you're not. This helps to give you an idea of the context, situation, and even people that may be connected to you either feeling or not feeling them. Once you know this, you will be better able to identify any patterns or triggers that may be causing your stress and overwhelm to manifest. I like to call this "recognition in reflection," because as you reflect, you begin to recognize which patterns are useful to your healing and which are not.

Staying curious and being judgment-free with yourself as you reflect is important. For one NICU mother from the USA of two pre-term pregnancies, reflecting without judgment led her to change her direction of travel professionally as her work was the product of her NICU story. She shared:

"There is some permission you have to give yourself when you're ready, that you can leave that story behind you. Being a preemie mom, having preemie kids, and trauma doesn't have to define you for the rest of your life."

What is important to note with this mother's reflection outcome was the permission she gave herself and the absence of self-judgment. The former gives you your power back, the latter gives you yourself back. This can be a similar outcome for you with stress and overwhelm. You can give yourself permission to mitigate, avoid, and/or better manage the situations, things, and even people who cause stress and overwhelm in your life. You can give yourself permission to heal.

EXPLORATION

Going back to the concept of compartmentalization being a form of separation, let's use this to explore and break down your stress and overwhelm further. One way to do this is to separate the positive versus negative aspects of these emotions, which gives you clarity and choice. In my coaching practice, I typically ask my clients what attracted or repelled them about a situation. Adjusting this to stress and overwhelm, I invite you to ask yourself:

- What and/or who triggers stress and overwhelm?
- What and/or who provides calmness?

One American NICU mother of a 24-week preterm infant was clear about her triggers when she shared:

"I try to be out of conversations where me being my full self [as a parent] won't be accepted because I find holding that back to be painful still."

Being able to identify what situations caused her stress and overwhelm allowed this mother to make informed choices that were healthy for her, and define what she could gravitate towards to lessen the emotions and their impact. For her, it was creating community. She described it in this way:

"I had a whole community of people. Some are family, chosen family, friends, but the thread that connects them all is that they are people who never lost sight of what we went through and always continued to check in."

A Bereaved mother from the USA shared finding what she called her "sitting in the yuck" tribe:

"My community is creating a safe place for me. They're recognizing and validating the loss by sitting in the yuck with me.

They're not trying to make it better but are making it better because they're not trying to tell me, 'Oh, it's time to get up and go now.' They are just sitting in the loss, grief, and sadness with me and validating that it's ok that I'm here and that it's not over tomorrow. They're going to be here and are ok with the messiness."

Singling out not only what could cause you stress and overwhelm but also what or who doesn't, as noted in the exploratory questions and parent examples above, helps minimize these emotions. It does this by nudging you to focus on and appreciate only one thing at a time versus several things at once, which we know can overwhelm any of us.

Examples of singling out could be

- The NICU parent zeroing in on the first time they held their baby weeks after being born,
- The bereaved parent focusing on the few precious seconds or minutes of breath their child had before they breathed their last, or
- The parent of a two-year-old child with special needs celebrating them sitting up alone for the first time, regardless of this milestone being delayed.

More specifically, singling out moves you closer towards healing from these emotions by doing three things:

- **Promoting presence:** When you stay in one moment of your experience, even if it is a memory, it anchors you. It also facilitates presence, which is the "state of existing and being in tune to the here and now." Parents I've interviewed have shared that there is something calming and soothing about being still and present.

- **Provides Protection:** It can shield and protect you from a barrage of overlapping and conflicting internal thoughts and feelings.
- **Mitigates overwhelm:** As mentioned previously, having fewer versus multiple emotional experiences to focus on automatically minimizes stress and overwhelm and is less work for your body, mind, and soul.

ACTION

Now, how do you make the lessons you have learned from your reflection and exploration stick? How do you better navigate these two emotions in a healthier and more sustainable way?

One coaching-based strategy I use is something I call *intentional refocusing*. This is a more detailed way to single something out and means your attention is focused on where you want to be with this emotion. You do this by answering the questions below:

- How will I know when I'm less stressed/overwhelmed?
- What will be different about my behavior when I'm less stressed/overwhelmed?

Your answer to these questions becomes your personal measuring tool to assist you in knowing when you're moving closer towards your goal and desired outcome of being and feeling less stressed and overwhelmed. It is measured by your new behavior and thoughts. For example, an American NICU and Bereaved mother of a 24-week preterm infant shared:

"I was being cautious and overprotective with my son, which caused me increased stress and worry. When he's going out and not with me or doing anything that has any potential danger,

such as playing sports, my mind would always go to, 'What if something happens?"

To change this narrative in her head and do something differently, per the second question above, she self-talked herself away from that mental space of stress to a space of knowing her son will be ok. She explained:

"I stop and remind myself that he needs to grow up and take risks, and I won't be with him all the time to protect him."

The latter way of allowing her son to take risks was her measuring tool informing her what her behavior and thoughts would be without stress or worry.

Journaling:

Grab a notebook or piece of paper and write down your answers to the following questions:

1. How does Stress and Overwhelm show up for you?
2. What do you want to change about Stress and Overwhelm in your life?
3. How will you know when you've achieved it? (i.e. What will you be doing, saying, thinking, or feeling differently than now).

Take time to write down any other thoughts that are coming up for you about Stress and Overwhelm.

SHOCK/DISBELIEF

Shock: A sudden, upsetting, or surprising event or experience.

Disbelief: An inability or refusal to accept that something is true or real.

"It was a really hard, quite a hard experience. We were sleeping while crying. My wife is carrying a dead baby inside, it was really personally draining. I don't know how to explain the emotions."

Above is the account of a Ugandan NICU and Bereaved father of preterm twins in which one died in utero at five months gestation and the other was born at six months gestation. His anguish and shock at what he was experiencing was so palpable that words failed him.

Shock and disbelief were typically the first emotions the parents I interviewed shared that they felt; 45% of the parents I interviewed expressed having this emotion. Although they mean slightly different things, parents I spoke to used them interchangeably during our conversations, similarly to how they spoke about the emotions stress and overwhelm. Hence, I will do the same here.

Combining the two definitions above results in this definition:

***A sudden, upsetting, or surprising event or experience
you can't believe is real or true.***

Being a NICU, Bereaved, or Special Needs Parent fits this definition to a tee. You are literally thrust into these unknown and scary worlds you didn't know existed, were not prepared for and could not believe you were inhabiting. I often described these spaces as surreal. Part of their surrealness is because they are so far removed from any semblance of what you would have thought parenting would be. The contrast between what you expected and what you received is stark. Consider the following:

- You expect to have a normal, 9-month uncomplicated, healthy pregnancy. You receive a 5-month pregnancy, a 1 pound. 1 ounce very sick baby.

- You expect to deliver your baby and go home soon afterwards. You receive a lengthy stay in the NICU, initially separated from your baby.

- You expect your baby to live. You receive a baby who is dead.

- You expect your child to develop normally. You receive a child with a range of additional and complex needs.

Any one of these scenarios can cause shock and disbelief. As previously mentioned throughout this book, because the NICU, Bereavement, and Special Needs worlds are frequently interconnected, parent's shock and disbelief emotions can feel like they're double and triple-fold. The magnitude of these types of experiences and the impression they leave on our brains and in our hearts can't be overstated. It feels like you're putting an x through what's normal and a check next to what's abnormal.

Trauma-Informed Specialist, Mary Coughlin describes the NICU space in this way:

"Being in the NICU is a departure from the normal developmental trajectory, emotionally, physically, spiritually, existentially."

As a Bereaved mother asked after her twins died:

"Is this really happening?"

A simple yet poignant question that captures the essence of these two interconnected emotions.

Several parents I interviewed shared how so unprepared emotionally and physically they were for this life-changing, traumatic event that as previously mentioned, some described it as like having an out-of-body experience. This is in alignment with the color blue relating to disconnection that Brad Hardie mentioned previously in the Trauma section of this book.

The vastness and vividness of their descriptions of their lived experiences with these emotions are important to take note of because it is a reminder that the manifestation of shock and disbelief can be so different for each person, and this is ok. In addition, given that these emotions tend to sometimes occur during the initial stage of the parent's lived experience, there are a multitude of other variables that may be involved in their story, such as hospital staff, healthcare professionals, etc.

Shock and disbelief can have a massive impact on NICU, Bereaved, and Special Needs parents, so you are not alone if you are struggling to come to grips with them along your parenting journey.

A NICU and Special Needs mother from Hungary described her NICU experience as:

"feeling like when you have to jump out from an airplane and you have no parachute at all. You are just falling."

Going back to the out-of-body experience description mentioned earlier, shock and disbelief can make you feel like you are a spectator of your own life. Sitting on the sidelines watching in horror as it all plays out. One NICU mother from the USA of a 24-week preterm infant likened it to a movie:

"I was not in control. It was like a movie scene with so many decisions being made around me about me."

Confusion can occur because of these emotions. A French NICU and Bereaved mother of preterm twins in which one lived and the other didn't shared how the shock and sadness of her experience left her confused during the traumatic experience of losing her child.

"I had a pain in my tummy all day and went back home. That same evening, I'm going to the bathroom and suddenly I have a baby going down into the toilet. That was my daughter. So, I have this baby and really didn't know what to do with her because I knew she was dead. It was really weird because my toddler son was playing in front of the bathroom and I had to grab a towel, wrap my dead daughter in the towel and hide her someway if I could. I then go out the bathroom with a big smile for my son."

These emotions can force you to have to function within two contrasting and simultaneous realities, so you can survive them both. Think back to the role of the amygdala which detects and helps you respond to danger by taking action. This mother acted 'normal' amid a traumatic situation, despite her not fully understanding or processing what was happening.

Shock and disbelief can sometimes occur after the traumatic event occurs. One American NICU mother of a 29-week preterm infant had such a traumatic delivery experience that she didn't fathom that she'd had a baby until days later, which shocked and surprised her. She vividly describes her delivery and its aftermath like this:

"In my head, I'm thinking they were doing a 3rd trimester abortion, and I was trying to think what that looked like. I thought they were chopping my baby up and taking him out. Then they closed me up and took me to recovery. I first met my son 4–5 days after I had him. This was when I knew he was alive and the first time I realized that there was an actual baby."

Shock and disbelief can produce an inability to process what was previously understood. Described in this way by an Australian NICU mother of 31-week preterm infant twins:

"The whole time you're trying to process that shock because, up until then, everything was going reasonably ok. Every time we hit a hiccup, it was fixed. This time, it wasn't."

Of course, these emotions don't just occur in the NICU or when experiencing Bereavement. Along the special needs journey, parents also expressed experiencing shock and disbelief, both when their child was initially diagnosed and equally when the penny dropped and there was a moment of realization that special needs would be a part of their journey and their lives forever. An example of this double-fold shock was explained in this way by an American NICU and Special Needs mother:

"You're told early on that there is a two-year catch-up period for developmental delays and somehow, they will just miraculously become like every other full term child. I believed that for a short while, but I've learned in 16 years that a micro preemie does not transform into a typically developing child. It just does not happen. I guess I wanted to believe that at the time, so there were definitely disappointments along the way when I realized, 'No, this is not a temporary thing. This is my life now. It's very important to become educated early on, understand the reality of your situation, and adjust your expectations accordingly."

A NICU and Special Needs father of a 32-week preterm infant from the USA described his penny-dropping moment as "an emotional journey."

He further explained this journey as:

"the realization that my child is changing from the NICU to Special Needs, and I'm having to change with him."

Lastly, as mentioned earlier, shock and disbelief can sometimes include other variables such as the healthcare professionals, which can further adversely impact the experience. A NICU, Bereaved, and Special Needs mother from Germany described the following scenario involving these added variables, as she was being wheeled into the delivery room.

"I was entering into the surgery room, and my husband was asked by the medical team, 'Who should survive? Who's the one who is most important?' Then they said to him, 'We cannot promise you if one or the three,' meaning me or either of my twins, 'will survive.' Then they left him standing there."

Let's pause and give space to these experiences. In all of them, there is a sense of jarring and rawness, which increases the magnitude of the parents' shock and disbelief. Although these are a small fraction of the stories shared with me, they provide a tiny glimpse into the worlds that NICU, Bereavement, and Special Needs parents have had to inhabit through no fault of their own. You may even see glimpses of your own story within theirs.

It is important to note that sometimes when people experience a sudden and traumatic event, like many of the parents I spoke with have, they may initially feel absolutely nothing, a numbness. Research has shown that this numbing aspect of shock and disbelief is a natural occurrence to help you process what has just happened at a pace you can manage, when you are ready. It can last for a few hours or a few days. Quickly tapping back into my former health and clinical background for a minute, from a medical perspective, shock is our body's response to a life-threatening situation. It causes our blood vessels to constrict or narrow in our hands and feet to conserve or protect the blood flow to our vital organs. It is doing this to keep you alive physically, much like I suppose numbness is keeping you alive emotionally.

As part of my coaching and consulting practice, I often lead and facilitate workshops and present as a public speaker on various topics. During a workshop presentation a few years ago, I did an icebreaker called the Island Mix-up. A quick synopsis of it is this:

Attendees are shown five islands and given a choice to select the one they want to live on. Beautiful islands such as Maui, The

Seychelles, etc. Easy enough, right? There is only one problem. One by one, each island will eventually sink into the sea, forcing the attendees to run to another one. Eventually, only one island will remain that they must live on. One they didn't choose, and is cold, frightening, and uninhabitable. They can't believe they are there.

This is the same with the NICU, Bereavement, or Special Needs spaces parents enter into. Their expected and chosen island, which is their expected birth or parenting experience, has sunk, and they're now on one that feels like a complete abyss. They can't get off of this unchosen island, which is now forever a part of them and their life story. They also can't believe they are there.

Sucker-punched, is a boxing term used to describe a punch thrown at the recipient that is unprovoked or when they are distracted, giving them no time to react, prepare, or defend themselves. This is how I think of the shock and disbelief emotions because there is an unexpected blow. This was true for me and my experience as a NICU, Bereaved, and Special Needs parent. Each experience overlapped one another making me feel like the rug was being swept out from under me. Pregnancy and infant loss—punch. Extremely preterm birth—punch. Secondary infertility—punch. Special Needs—punch. Each time, I couldn't breathe. Each time, I couldn't comprehend my reality. Each time, it felt like the wind was knocked out of me. Each time, I was sucker-punched.

The lingering impact of those moments for me are the following: no longer believing that you are "safe" once you reach your second trimester, forever grieving my son's twin and his three other siblings who are not here, having twinges of hurt realizing my son will never see my face.

Although I don't stay in these moments and am grateful for what I have, they have forever shaped my perspective and are a part of my parenting DNA. Nothing or no one prepares you for it, and even if they tried to prepare you, you still would not be.

REFLECTION

As we have seen thus far, Shock and Disbelief can shake us to our core and color and affect our perspective of the world around us, both during and after the traumatic event. As part of our initial stage of reflection, let's reflect on these aspects together through the story of a Bereaved mother of 20-week twins who both died.

[During Traumatic Event]

"I'd called the doctors that morning, the day before the babies were born and told them what I was feeling. That I felt like I was having contractions and was worried that I might be in labor. They told me, 'Oh, it's nothing, it sounds like Braxton Hicks so just lay down for a while, and if they pick up, then come in.' I wasn't given any clear advice. It was just a wait and see. We finally went to the hospital, and they found out I'd dilated and said there was nothing they could do. At that point, I basically knew what was going to happen—that they were going to die. I just didn't know how quickly it would happen."

[Post Traumatic Event]

"I don't trust doctors anymore. If they tell me something, I'm like, 'Ok, prove it to me,' instead of just accepting them at their word."

Further reflection, discussion, and inquiry about her experience and response to it were done, particularly around how her experience has shaped her. One question I was curious about was:

How does shock and disbelief impact who you are?

For this mother, it both adversely and positively impacted her belief system. From a negative perspective, because she was not believed or taken seriously by the medical staff the day before she lost her babies, she no longer believes any medical staff or professional. She shared that her mistrust of them had become integrated into how she showed up as a person and parent.

Positively, her self-belief became more developed. Her words were: *"I trust my gut a lot more."* This in turn gave her more power and control back from a situation in which she felt powerless and out of control.

Peeling back the layers of how an emotion can and does impact you is a big part of your healing. It increases your awareness, but even more significantly, it gives you clarity, guidance, and ownership of how you want to manage that emotion in the future in a way that serves you best. Sometimes with shock and disbelief, it does not feel possible to manage it because of the surrealness of it, but it can be done, as the example above shows.

EXPLORATION

I mentioned previously about numbness being a healthy compartmentalization for shock and disbelief situations. I propose another way to compartmentalize them in a healthy way—be objective. Two exploratory-type questions that can help, and I invite you to consider are:

1. What is one thing about shock and disbelief you feel you could manage or control?
2. In what ways could you do this?

Breaking it down in this way helps to:

- Tackle one challenge or conflict *before* you do another one, or
- Put one thing to the side *in order* to tackle the other.

Returning to the Bereaved mother's experience again, this breaking-it-down process manifested for her in the following way:

"Being a nurse, I kind of took the emotions out of it to process it. One of the things I said was, 'Ok, God, if you're going to take my babies, take them now. Don't get them to viability and have them poked and prodded and then die anyway.' I didn't want us to stay there in the hospital for three weeks thinking we're going to make it and have them suffer and then take them anyways."

In this mother's story, being objective allowed her to get through the awful evitability of losing her babies because she knew for her, having them suffer would have been worse. This situation shows the benefits of compartmentalization in certain situations. Trying to process it all in one go would have been overwhelming.

ACTION

Taking action with shock and disbelief involves sitting with these interconnected emotions for a while and further reflecting on how they are showing up for you. This helps you determine what your next step should be. As you do so, be gentle with yourself, no self-judgment, and remember that there is no right or wrong answer. The only right answer is the one that makes sense for you, where you are, and where you want to be along your emotional journey.

I invite you to consider the following questions about shock/disbelief in your life:

1. What resonates with you when you're experiencing shock and disbelief?
2. What is that telling you about where you are with these emotions?
3. What do you need to suspend or stop?
4. What is one thing you can focus on?
5. Who do you need to assist you?

Journaling:

Get your notebook or piece of paper and write down your answers to the following questions:

1. How does Shock and Disbelief show up for you?
2. What do you want to change about Shock and Disbelief in your life?
3. How will you know when you've achieved it? (i.e. What will you be doing, saying, thinking, or feeling differently than now).

Write down any other thoughts that are coming up for you about Shock and Disbelief.

HOPE (THE CAROUSEL)

Hope: An optimistic state of mind that is based on an expectation of positive outcomes in a person's life.

As we come to the final part of our journey together through this book, I want celebrate and thank you for caring about your emotional healing and wellness enough to walk through this emotional landscape with me. Thank you for being open to exploring the psychosocial hills and valleys of your lived experience as a NICU, Bereaved, and Special Needs parent. I encourage you to keep in mind and revisit the concepts discussed and explored as you continue to build up, replenish, and nourish your emotional resilience and health.

Going from Rollercoasters to Carousels

As mentioned previously, parents in the NICU, Bereaved, and Special Needs spaces, frequently describe their experiences as feeling like they are on a rollercoaster. Complete with those jarring and unexpected dips, flips, and twirls of a rollercoaster ride, which can be unpleasant and scary. Marketed as "fun," I have never quite understood why these monstrous fear-inducing rides were billed as such and why we buy into the myth that they are. I can count on three fingers the number of times I have been on a rollercoaster and the same number of times I wished I hadn't gone. I must have missed the "fun" memo because it most definitely was not. Anyhow, I digress.

The point is we choose, naively or not, to go on a rollercoaster. We do not choose to be a NICU, Bereaved, or Special Needs parent.

While our emotional journey can often feel like a continuous rollercoaster ride, one that we don't seem to have control of, the aim and trajectory of this book is to get you off this ride and onto another one which I propose is a better one: The Carousel.

As I shared in the Preface, I chose this ride as a symbol of our destination because although the carousel is still moving, it does so at a slower, calmer pace. It feels more controlled and less scary, and if there is an unexpected dip, it is not as deep, so you are more able to manage it. Events, situations and stuff will still move or affect you emotionally as you go throughout your life. My wish for you as you do so, is to to find a way to manage your emotions in a calmer, healthier, more intentional, and dare I say, joyful, manner.

When on the rollercoaster, you are not able to process what is happening to you. Remember, processing simply means having the ability to deal with something. This can take a bit of time to get to within your emotional journey because when you are in that acute NICU, Bereaved, or Special Needs stage, you often have no capacity to deal with anything but are literally just trying to survive one second at a time. I still have vivid memories imbedded in my brain of when our son was born. Namely, the:

- Anesthesiologist standing at the top of my head gently and calmly telling me that our son was here "but very tiny,"
- Cling-clang of the surgical instruments,
- Pushing/pulling sensation and pressure of the surgeons on my lower abdomen during the emergency C-section as they worked to get my son out,
- Rushing sound of the NICU team racing to my right side outside of my view as they frantically worked on him,
- Me waiting to hear a whimper, sigh, or any sound of life that would tell me that he was alive, and
- After several minutes, which felt like hours, a nurse telling my husband that he "could see him."

I did not process any of that until many years later. When I did, I could appreciate the magnitude of my emotional experience on many levels and draw strength from it.

Likewise, you are also capable of processing or breaking through whatever emotions you feel are blocking or preventing you from showing up in the manner that you want. It takes time to get off that constant emotional rollercoaster and onto a more manageable carousel, because:

Processing is a process.

I invite you to allow yourself time, space, and grace to go through it. The very fact that you have this book in your hands tells me that you want to go through the process of a getting off that traumatic, emotional rollercoaster. I hope this book has helped you start to do that.

My son's journey reminds me daily that the heart sees what the eyes can't. Similarly, I want to remind you that hope prevails amidst the pain. You may not see or feel it all the time, but it is there, which reminds me of one of my favorite poets, the late Maya Angelou who said:

> *Just like moon and like suns,*
> *With the certainty of tides,*
> *Just like hope springing high,*
> *Still, I'll rise.*
> *(Excerpt from Still I Rise, by Maya Angelou)*

You can and will rise.

Hence, I leave you with the hope, knowledge, and tools to do so throughout your ongoing emotional journey, and your life. I'm not leaving you on your own though and am sharing the following:

1. **Words of Advice, Appendix 1.** A collection of parent-to-parent heartfelt and insightful tips, words of wisdom and

encouragement to you from all the parents I interviewed around the world. Personal reminders that you are not alone.

2. **Resources, Appendix 2** (Organized by Continent and Country). A comprehensive range of resources of organizations, products, and services I've collated from around the globe. Collectively, they provide you with a wealth of relevant and useful information and support. I know most of the people behind them personally, so feel free to reach out to them and tell them that I sent you.

Lastly, to continue your 'Carousel' journey of growth and development, I invite and encourage you to do the following:

- Continue to be committed to your emotional healing.
- Revisit the emotions and strategies discussed in this book.
- Use the journaling space to reflect on any new insights to move you forward.
- Read the words of encouragement from parents like you in the Words of Advice (Appendix 1).
- Browse through the range of resources provided and reach out to them (Appendix 2).
- Feel free to reach out to me
- Don't stop. As the late civil rights activist Martin Luther King, Jr. said during a 1960 speech he gave at Spelman College:

"If you can't fly, then run. If you can't run, then walk. If you can't walk, then crawl. Whatever you do, you have to keep moving forward".

WORDS OF ADVICE

(Parents to Parent)
From Roller Coasters to Carousels

Advocacy

- *"Only you can navigate this. You have to do your research, educate the people who don't understand it and very succinctly put into words what your child needs."*

- *"You are the expert of your child and always will be."*

- *"As parents, we have a role to teach professionals the potential of our child because they may only see their condition or diagnosis. Our child is one more statistic."*

- *"Don't let a diagnosis stop your child."*

- *"Know what you need and when you need it."*

- *"Ask as many questions as you feel is necessary. Don't be afraid to ask everything that pops in your head, but in the same regard, be prepared that there may not be an answer yet. The questions you ask can trigger thought processes. It isn't a disappointment when there aren't answers, it's a learning moment."*

- *"Don't be afraid to ask questions or write everything out. My NICU nurses thought I was crazy because of the journals that I kept, but I'm so grateful that I did."*

- *"Believe in yourself, your power to comfort your child and be an advocate in whatever way. To be an advocate you will create your new normal and you will be ok."*

Ask For Help

- *"Get connected to resources and ask for help. Be that squeaky wheel. Networking is really important"*

- *"Ask for the support you need, if you can articulate and think about this"*

- *"Be ok to say, I need help, or can you help me and be able to explain, how they can help you. A lot of people don't know how to help, so it's best to express your needs so they know how. Also, seek professional help to make sure it doesn't fester."*

Be Adaptable

- *"Have conviction with what you're doing and realize that sometimes you're going to make decisions that are the wrong decisions. Learn from them. Pride can't get in the way. I'm using 13+years of what I'm learning from my kid, and here is the delightfully infuriating part: What was working great for 6 months may not be right anymore and you have to completely change your step and that's just part of the process. Adaptability as the parent of a special needs child is absolutely crucial. The not knowing, realizing that it might take a while to know how or if your child will be independent as an adult, and coming to grips and accepting that [is hard]. This one thought can lead to five hundred."*

Every Journey is Unique

- *"Every NICU stay and journey is different; it doesn't matter the length of your stay, whether it's 12 weeks, 12 days, or 12 hours, it changes the vision of what you thought becoming a parent would be. So, any emotion you have tied to that is valid and real, and you're allowed to feel them. Just because I spent 12 weeks and you spent 12 hours, that is still the NICU and that is not the norm. No one knows the NICU exists going through those doors. That What To Expect When You're Expecting book, there's a section at the back about 'when something goes wrong'. Nobody reads that part because they think, 'It's not going to happen to me, that happens to other people'. Suddenly you're like, wait what? You're that other person. "*

- *"The journey is yours. There is no roadmap, so you get to pick the direction it goes in. You may have the same journey as someone else but might walk it differently or at a different pace."*

- *"Don't be judged by other people about how you deal with the situation. Don't negate yourself. You're resilient and have it in you; you take each minute as it comes."*

Finding Joy Through the Pain

- *"As painful, sad, and difficult as it is, it's going to change your life, make you stronger, help you find your joy. Have to look for the lights and reasons for the light. I'm a better person because of what happened. You carry your sadness, but it brings huge joy and gratitude. You can always find positives."*

- *"Have a sense of humour about everything."*

- *"It's hard to think there's meaning in so much pain, but there is."*

Finding Your Community of Support (aka Your Tribe)

- *"Time heals. Try to find some people to join you on the rollercoaster because you do feel like you're on your own. I once described this as a ski lift – there are times you need people in your carriage and there are other times you need them left behind. Sometimes, you've got to put people outside of your carriage and that's hard."*

- *"Tap into our reserves. Sometimes we don't even know that we have them. When you're thrown into something, having your tribe of people around you to lift you up is important but also to be in your own space as well."*

- *"Really important that you connect with your child and reach out to others who've been on that journey because the isolation creates so many negative experiences. If there is someone there who can support and enlighten you, it can change the experience of your journey."*

- *"Get you a good support system, whether it's your friends or family. Not someone who wants to make your experience about themselves."*

- *"If your circle isn't doing it for you, get a new circle. This is the time that your community is supposed to embrace and love you and if there is an empty seat at that table, [get others] to fill it for you. During my [illness], for the first time in my life, my table changed, and I wasn't even sad about it because I was so busy trying to not die. I saw people exiting my circle and I was like, "Bye" because I didn't have time. Interestingly enough, although my table got a little smaller, the quality of who was sitting at my table was really great. It may not even be the people you thought or expected to be there."*

- *"Sympathy goes nowhere except to the broken neck syndrome (i.e. That's so sad, we're going to talk about this for a while and y'all tell me if she needs anything). You can't have action, if you don't have compassion and empathy. You want compassionate and empathetic people who take action and are willing to get in the game of hard with you. Not the person wearing the t-shirt which says on the back: 'Friend available, but I don't do hard'."*

- *"I think we also get stuck into the idea that we just have to have one circle [of support], and everyone has to fit into that circle and that's all we have, but really, we're a lot better if we have multiple circles. We have our family, and nothing changes that, but they can't meet all our needs always and that's ok. The more we're loved the better off we are, and people love in different ways. You may have your work circle and hopefully will have some real authentic relationships there you can count on. Then your social circle. If you've got 2 or 3 really good people [in your circles] that's golden."*

- *"Find some support to help you through it [grief]. I needed to talk to somebody because this experience was bigger than me and bigger than anything I could handle on my own."*

- *"It seems obvious, but surround yourself with family and friends, even if it's not your nature. I'm kind of a lonely person, but in that situation, you need to be able to talk, either to a professional or family or friends, or people in the same situation, but talk. Get help that's coming from any kind of way."*

- *"Really think it's about seeking community and support and not trying to bottle it all up and make your way through it. It's about understanding that you are going through a traumatic time and not discounting that. I really feel like I discounted that and just focused on the baby and tried to be tough and get through it, but you really have to take care of yourself so you can take care of the baby. Many marriages have failed and so many parents are still struggling."*

- *"Find community resources. I wish I had connected more with a parent community earlier on because it's been one of the most singular important things is to do is to find your people. Somebody else that is facing or going through it too. However, you can find your people, do it because although your family and friends are always going to be there for you, they're never going to get it the way someone who's had that lived experience will."*

Get Professional Support

- *"To realise [our children] came here when they came here for this reason, for us to teach, learn and know and God willing continue to learn, however that works out. So, getting the help as soon as you can; and understanding and doing so is the very best thing you can do for your child."*

- *"I recommend that moms and dads see a therapist because although dads don't experience the physical loss [of the baby], they're still hurting and still need support just like moms do."*

- *"Your healing is just as important as the medical care your children need. All those lists of specialists on that list of essentials should also have your mental health on it. Whether that's peer mentoring, coaching, counselling, psychiatric help, etc. make sure you take care of your own self."*

- *"I remember one time describing the NICU journey as being like trudging through mud with boots made of lead. That's how I felt going through life every day. You don't just have to learn how to cope with that. There are ways for recovery, healing, wholeness, and joy; but you have to have your mental health taken care of to get to that point, It doesn't happen spontaneously."*

Hope

- *"I really want people to know that there is hope. This is not the end of the line; this is not your forever. There are many more chapters to be written."*

- *"I felt so out of control in the NICU, but I chose to be hopeful and positive, although there were many days I didn't feel that way. I also feel that babies feel your energy, so I was thinking, what kind am I giving to this child. It's weird how you kind of figure out some sort of way to anchor you."*

- *"You are not alone."*

- *"This is not the club that anyone would ask to join but you come out of it knowing that you are stronger than you ever imagined you could be and that your child will teach you things that you couldn't have learned any other way."*

- *"Share with your child the details in their experience. it's an opportunity for them to take pride in their experience. I think it's important for children to be aware of what they went through, how they've overcome it and to understand their uniqueness in that way. To see it as something that makes them special, and speaks to their resilience, strength, and power. It's one way of flipping the experience from something that's negative to something that's empowering and positive and meaningful, beneficial to the parents and the child."*

- *"Try as much as you can to find reasons to have hope. Hold onto whatever positives you can find in the experience or the future because that's what's going to get you through. Connect to the strength and motivation to do all you can do to build a better future for yourself and your baby."*

Living with Loss/Bereavement

- *"Go to a counsellor who has experienced loss. Some hospital groups are there for people who want clinical answers and there is a place for that. My experience has been a lot of hospital support groups are run by professionals who get paid a little extra to do it and they've never lost a baby. They may have been with tons of families but never experienced loss."*

- *"As parents, we have to set the standard that our child, the one we lost, will always be our child and a part of our family and will never be forgotten. It's ok for you to talk about him/her. I want you to. This is your new life."*

- *"Surround yourself with other bereaved families, via an in person or online support group to connect with other families. The stories may be different, but the outcome is the same. As bereaved moms we get it, we know. A lot of [the support] is unspoken."*

- *"To grieving parents, allow yourself time to feel whatever you feel. There isn't an established beginning and end point. The stages of grief aren't linear. You can hit one [stage] and then go back and keep going back and back until however long. Don't let anyone tell you that you should be over it by now. No, I'm not ever going to be over it."*

- *"Find families who've experienced the same thing. Group support was such a lifesaver for me; I may not be where I am today without that community."*

- *"I suggest, because it helps with the healing, once they're ready, to find some way to honour that baby/babies whether it's doing a walk or making blankets and donating them to the NICU. Something that you can do to keep the memories of that baby alive instead of just tucking it into a box and putting it on a shelf."*

- *"It's ok to grieve differently. Sometimes one parent lets go and the other holds on. Neither is better or worse but sometimes if you're the person letting go, the person who's not feels like you're doing something wrong, not realizing that your love for your child isn't any less. You're just manifesting it differently."*

Nurture Your Marriage/Partnership Relationship

- *"If you have a spouse, partner, etc, don't forget them. Your partnership is just as important as caring for your child, in order to show up as parents. In order to be in the moment, you sometimes have to take a step back even if it's a 5-10 mental health break to rejuvenate. Those little moments are important."*

Practical Support (Give/Receive)

- *"The way I work in my teaching practice, is to work in the very practical and very profound realms. In the practical realm a person may say, 'Oh my neighbour just had a baby, a medically fragile child and is in the hospital. What should I do?' I'm like, put a case of water in the back of the car or fill up individual snack bags with nuts and protein because they're in survival mode and are not going to be giving themselves these things."*

- *"Like a marathon: You need people who are giving you food, literally and emotionally, you need someone who is cheering you on (an expert or your best friend). When you fall down, you need someone who will come and pick you up, take you away for a few minutes so you can restart. Someone to run with you, keeping your same rhythm."*

Reflection

- *"It's important to journal. When [my twins] were born, before we knew about [my son who would pass], I'd been writing in their books. After he passed, I wrote down the whole journey, (i.e. how much he weighed, my expectations not being met, etc.). It was very coherent, I was talking to myself, also gave me permission to have a safe space when I was angry. You can say things in your journal that you can't say aloud and won't get judged for. Regardless of whether you read it again or not."*

- *"I think it depends on where you are in your journey (i.e. In NICU, pregnant, loss, post-loss, post-NICU, trying to get pregnant, totally burnt out, etc.). Try to envision where do you want to be/do in 2-5 years. For me, my vision was to have a happy family living at home and this helped us figure out what the priorities were."*

- *"To acknowledge, that what parents in this situation are facing is one of the most traumatic experiences that anyone can undergo and it's a terrifying and lonely place to be, to have to contemplate this limbo between birth and death. At the same time, I truly believe that it can also be one of the most life-affirming and transformative experiences that we can have, and it's crucial to recognize both."*

- *"You can process your grief and experiences in a lot of ways, but you don't need to start your own non-profit, because you're giving yourself a lot of work in order to give back. It seems like people go through the NICU and start a non-profit to go make baskets. It's probably a repressed grief or trauma situation, but you don't need to build something that will require a lot of time, energy, and capacity, for it to fizzle after 1 or 2 years."*

- *"If something hurts, it's ok to step back, take care of yourself, and do whatever you need to do in that moment to get through it. Give yourself the grace to do it. My tattoo is one breath. When things get rough, I ask myself, how can I get through the rest of my life? By focusing on one breath at a time. The rest will take care of itself."*

Resilience

- *"It is a journey and there are peaks and valleys; recognizing the natural waves of life and that there are peaks and valleys; when you say journey, to me, it's like a hike, you're going through a forest, around a lake, etc., our life is not a straight trajectory and for some it is or may seem to be but for the most of us, it's a journey"*

- *"I do believe whatever happens to us does make us a stronger person. There is a song by the singer Pink, which says, you're bent. Not broken. It's important for us to remember that. I do think that the more life experiences come our way, the stronger we get, I would hope so."*

- *"You're stronger than you think you are. Human beings are incredible; keep going/they rise up."*

Self-Compassion

- *"Take care of yourself, others, and your partner."*

- *"Be kind to yourself. When we're in the moment [of the NICU], we don't think about ourselves. You're no good to anyone else if you can't function, so get water, food, etc."*

- *"Just breathe and then look at the other things you can think about that day. The hardest part of the NICU is the waiting, and you live that uncertainty for a long time."*

- *"Self-care doesn't have to be complicated. I used to think that it meant you to take a day off; find a babysitter, go get nails done, journal, etc.- all this stuff we're told. It is ok to sit outside of your porch with a coffee or stay up 5 minutes longer and just do nothing, sit in the car and cry, or walk really slowly to the mailbox. It shouldn't be something you have to make and build time into your day for because that is overwhelming in itself. It's hard to for me to remember to eat lunch, so I can't say, 'Oh I'm going to take care of myself today as it won't happen. That moment when your child is quiet, falls asleep, in the toilet, etc., its ok to just be."*

- *"When I mentor moms, including checking in the baby, family, I also asks things like: Were you able to get out for walk today, read something you wanted to for 10 minutes. That self-care is so important and it's not something I allowed myself to do [in the NICU]. It's ok to sleep another 15 minutes and arrive to the NICU 30 min later than yesterday. Be kind to yourself because you're going through a lot too. Give yourself grace."*

- *"You're not broken and there is biological proof of that. Traumatic stress is a protective response, a survival response, and your body did what it needed to do to survive what you survived."*

- *"If you want your child to heal, you have to take care of yourself. It's profound to really be conscious and aware of your own energy and how you show up as much as you are able."*

- *"Know that you did nothing wrong. Whatever happened is not your fault."*

- *"It's ok to put yourself first, even when you don't want to. I'm good when someone gives me a task and I see it written down. If someone had given me a selfcare checklist, I would've done it."*

- *"Best advice is what was given to me: Be kind to yourself. It's one of those things that you forget. Take each day as it comes."*

Sharing Your Feelings

- *"Don't be afraid to talk about your emotions to others/partners; nor feel scared or ashamed about talking about the help you need. Talking to other communities with same experiences, like peer groups, remind you that you are not alone."*

- *"Do not be afraid to share with those people closest to you how you're really feeling; My mom is my person but [instead of talking to her about how I was feeling], I would snap at her because for me anxiety and fear comes out as anger. We've had lots of conversations afterwards and she said that she knew I wasn't mad at her. All the research about divorce being so prevalent after loss because those emotions come out in different ways. Don't be ashamed to find your people, those you're comfortable with and can share your deepest feelings."*

- *"Speak your emotion. Whatever it is, just speak it. You can be angry, sad, joyful, happy all within a minute; Find your people or tribe that allow you to just be that."*

Staying Present

- *"Stay present, in the now. This moment is pretty much all you have. When you are so present, you don't have to fear. You become the eye of the storm and stay calm, can ground yourself. I came to understand this upon reflection after the NICU; always thinking about the future but now is now; what I have today. If I'm going through the storm, stop, I only have control of this moment. When I was writing my book, was when I was doing a lot of reflecting."*

- *"Don't be a fixer. Learn to love your child, yourself, your situation."*

Trust Your Instincts

- *"In the NICU, you know your baby. Listen to your parental instincts and don't ever let anyone tell you that you can't share it. If you didn't say it and something happens to your child, you will live with the guilt forever."*

RESOURCES

Organized by Continent/Country

NORTH AMERICA	ORGANIZATION
Canada (National)	**Canadian Premature Babies Foundation** – www.cpbf-fbpc.org - A parent led, charitable organisation providing education, support and advocacy for premature babies and their families.
Mexico (National)	**Con Amor Venceras (CAV)** – https://conamorvenceras.org – Provides support of premature babies and their families through creating awareness, dissemination of information, research and development.
USA (National)	1. **NICU Parent Network (NPN)** – www.nicuparentnetwork.org – The premier national professional organisation of NICU Parent Leaders who collectively represent the needs and best interests of NICU families across the USA. 2. **National Perinatal Association (NPA) - https://www.nationalperinatal.org** – A national organisation promoting evidence-based practices in perinatal care.

NORTH AMERICA	ORGANIZATION
	3. **Hand To Hold** - https://handtohold. org - A nonprofit organisation that offers support groups, mentoring, counselling, and resources to parents of babies in the neonatal intensive care unit (NICU). 4. **PreemieWorld Foundation Inc.** – https://preemieworld.org - A nonprofit organization dedicated to improving the lives of families with patient education and practical help by creating equitable access of underserved populations to patient education, advocacy tools and outcomes data specific to the preemie population. 5. **Mommies Enduring Neonatal Death (M.E.N.D.)** – https://www.mend.org – A Christian nonprofit organization that reaches out to families who have suffered the loss of a baby through miscarriage, stillbirth, or early infant death. 6. **The NEC Society** – https://necsociety. org - A nonprofit organization dedicated to building a world without necrotizing enterocolitis (NEC) through research, advocacy, and education. 7. **Once Upon A Preemie, Inc** – https:// www.onceuponapreemie.org - A Black women-ed non-profit organization committed to pioneering solutions for neonatal equity to center Black preemie family experiences.

NORTH AMERICA	ORGANIZATION
	8. **Ruvelle** – https://ruvelle.com – The only truly trauma-informed company dedicated to improving high-risk pregnancy outcomes and reducing the risk of preterm birth by filling the gaps left by the medical and mental health fields with science-backed somatic and trauma-responsive support with health and health care. 9. **March of Dimes** – https://www.marchofdimes.org – A non-profit organization that fights for the health of all moms and babies in the USA. 10. **Hope for HIE** – https://www.hopeforhie.org – The premier organization connecting families, worldwide, through a comprehensive support network. 11. **The PPROM Foundation** – https://www.aapprom.org – A non-profit organization and public charity to provide resources and support for those experiencing Preterm Premature Rupture of Membranes (PPROM) in pregnancy and beyond.
Connecticut	**The Tiny Miracles Foundation** – https://www.ttmf.org – A non-profit organization with a mission to help families of infants born prematurely in Fairfield County, CT and beyond.

NORTH AMERICA	ORGANIZATION
Florida	1. **ICU Baby** – https://www.icubaby.org - A non-profit organization that provides financial, emotional, and informational support to NICU families in Miami and other areas. 2. **Silvie Bells** – https://silviebells.com – A non-profit organization that brings cheer to the families of sick and preemie babies in the NICU
Louisiana	**Saul's Light** – https://www.saulslight.org – A New Orleans-based nonprofit that provides support and community to families with babies in the neonatal intensive care unit (NICU).
New York area	**Maria's Hope** – https://mariashope.net – A parent-based volunteer organization that provides emotional support and mentoring services to parents with babies in the NICU at Maria Fareri Children's Hospital at Westchester Medical Center.
North Dakota	**Dear NICU Mama** – https://www.dearnicumama.com – A nonprofit and global community that provides immediate peer support to NICU mothers and their families through diverse programs and services.
Ohio	**Project NICU** – https://www.projectnicu.com – A nonprofit organization designed around peer support to families and the NICU community.
Pennsylvania	**Lily's Hope Foundation** – https://www.lilyshopefoundation.org – A nonprofit organization that answers the emergency needs of families with premature babies in the NICU

NORTH AMERICA	ORGANIZATION
Texas	**NICU Helping Hands** – https://nicuhelpinghands.org - A non-profit organization based in Fort Worth, Texas, that develops hospital- and community-based projects to provide education and support for families with babies in the neonatal intensive care unit (NICU), during their transition from hospital to home and in the event of an infant loss
SOUTH AMERICA	**ORGANIZATION**
Brazil **(National)**	**ONG Prematuridade** – https://prematuridade.com – The Brazilian Association of Parents, Relatives, Friends, and Caregivers of Premature Babies is the only national nonprofit organization dedicated to preventing preterm birth and ensuring the rights of premature babies and their families across Brazil.
EUROPE	**ORGANIZATION**
Europe **(Pan-European)**	**The European Foundation for the Care of Newborn Infants (EFCNI)** – https://www.efcni.org – The first pan-European organization and network to represent the interests of preterm and newborn infants and their families.
Bulgaria	**Our Premature Children Foundation** – https://premature-bg.com – A nonprofit organization providing support for premature babies and their families.
Czech Republic	**Nedoklubko** - https://www.nedoklubko.cz – A nonprofit organization supporting families of premature babies and neonatal wards in the Czech Republic.

EUROPE	ORGANIZATION
France	**SOS Prema** – https://www.sosprema.com – The Association supporting families of premature babies by several missions and fighting to give all premature children the best chance of growing up well.
Greece	**Ilitominon** – https://ilitominon.org – Founded by parents of premature babies to support families of premature babies and contribute to better neonatal care.
Hungary	**Melletted A Helyem** – https://www.mellettedahelyem.hu – The association for preterm care aimed at reducing the number of premature births in Hungary and improving the healthy survival rate of premature babies.
Ireland	**Irish Neonatal Health Alliance** – https://www.inha.ie – Ireland's first collaborative platform and network to represent the interests of preterm infants, ill infants in the Neonatal Intensive Care Units (NICUS), and their families.
Lithuania	**Neisnesiotukas** - https://www.neisnesiotukas.lt – A nonprofit associations for premature newborns and unites them, their parents, guardians, sponsors, and doctors.
Portugal	**XXS** – https://xxs-prematuros.com – The Portuguese Association to support premature babies.
Spain	**Prematura** - https://prematura.info – The Association of families of premature babies.
The Netherlands	**TAPS Support** - https://tapssupport.com – A registered charity dedicated to changing the way monochorionic twin pregnancies are diagnosed, handled, and treated, as well as raising the profile of Twin Anemia Polycythemia Sequence (TAPS)

EUROPE	ORGANIZATION
Turkey	**El Bebek Gül Bebek Association** – The Association of premature babies and their families, who carry out necessary studies for all premature babies to have a healthy future.
Ukraine	**Early Birds** – https://ranniptashky.org/ua - The Association of Parents of Premature Babies helps every premature child and their family to receive the highest level of medical, psychological, and social support to exercise their rights and freedoms.
United Kingdom (National)	1. **Bliss** – https://www.bliss.org.uk – Bliss supports parents and families of babies in neonatal care. 2. **Tommy's** – https://www.tommys.org – The UK's largest charity for pregnancy and baby loss, funding research and providing information and support. 3. **Child Bereavement UK** – https://www. childbereavementuk.org – Provides counselling, support groups, and resources for children, young people, parents, and families who have lost a chid or are grieving. 4. **Footprints Baby Loss** – https:// wwwfootprintsbabyloss.org – Provides vital support to bereaved families following the death of a baby or babies from a twin, triplet, or higher order multiple pregnancy, before, during, or after birth. 5. **The Butterfly Project** – https://www. neonatalbutterflyproject.org – Working to better understand the lived experience of families suffering baby loss in a multiple pregnancy, where at least one baby survives.

AFRICA	ORGANIZATION
Ghana	**African Foundation for Premature Babies and Neonatal Care (AFPNC)** – https://www.afpncvoice.org - The first pan-African organization and network to represent the interests of premature/sick babies and their families.
Uganda	**Preterm Infants Parents Network Uganda** – https://pipnu.org – A registered charity organization formed to offer support to families of premature babies.
Tanzania	**Doris Mollel Foundation (DMF)** - https://www.dorismollelfoundation.org – The first and onlhy NGO organization catering to the needs of premature babies in Tanzania.
ASIA	ORGANIZATION
Japan	**The Japanese Organization for NICU Families (JOIN)** - https://www.join.or.jp – A network connecting children and families nationwide by working with family associations in Japan.
OCEANIA	ORGANIZATION
Australia	**Miracle Babies Foundation** – https://www.miraclebabies.org.au – Australia's leading organization supporting families with a premature or sick newborn.
INTERNATIONAL	PRODUCTS/SERVICES
	1. **Caring Essentials Collaborative** – https://www.caringessentials.net – Internationally recognized leader in trauma-informed developmental care education for those who serve babies, children, and their families across all settings.

INTERNATIONAL	PRODUCTS/SERVICES
	2. **The Zaky (Nurtured By Design)** – https://thezaky.com – Human-Centered Ergonomics and Safety Engineering and Technology for Parent/Child
	3. **Pregnancy Brain** (book by Parijat Deshpande) – A Mind-Body Approach to Stress Management during a High-Risk Pregnancy
	4. **The Preemie Parent's Guide to Survival in the NICU** (book by Deb Discenza and Nicole Conn)
	5. **Tiny Humans, Big Lessons** (book by Sue Ludwig) – How the NICU Taught Me to Live with Energy, Intention and Purpose
	6. **Girl In Glass** (book by Deanna Fei) – How my "Distressed Baby" Defied the Odds, Shamed a CEO, and Taught Me the Essence of Love, Heartbreak, and Miracles.
	7. **Me Two Books** – https://www.metwobooks.com – Mission to create products that provide support, encouragement, and information for families, featuring preemie/NICU babies, twins, kids with disabilities, and those not represented by the traditional publishing industry.
	8. **Now I Lay Me Down To Sleep** – https://wwwnowilaymedowntosleep.org – A nonprofit organization that offers free professional portraiture to parents who lost a baby (USA)

INTERNATIONAL	PRODUCTS/SERVICES
	9. **Remember My Baby -** https://remembermybaby.org.uk – A UK-based registered charity that offers a free gift of baby remembrance photography to UK parents who lose their baby before, during, or shortly after birth. 10. **Speaking for Moms and Babies Inc** – https://jenniferdegl.com – Public Education on neonatal health issues. 11. **Families Blossoming LLC/GKF Coaching and Consulting** https://familiesblossoming.com - Separate yet related entities, providing a dual-focus on leadership and the NICU community, respectively. Focus areas of leadership and organisational wellness, trauma-informed coaching, NICU/maternal-infant health, diversity, empowerment, consulting and training/facilitation. 12. **For the Love of Babies** (book by Dr. Sue Hall) - One Doctor's Stories About Life in the Neonatal ICU. 13. **Trauma-Informed Care in the NICU** (book by Mary Coughlin) - Evidenced-Based Practice Guidelines for Neonatal Clinicians 14. **Moving the Human Spirit** – https://www.movingthehumanspirit.com – Trauma-Informed certification, training, and courses.

— APPENDIX 3 —

REFERENCES

1. Chow, S., Chow, R., Popovic, M., Lam, M.,Popovic, M., Merrick, J., Margalit, R.N., Lam, H., Milakovic, M., Chow, E., Popovic, J., (2015), Frontiers in Public Health, https://www.ncbi.nlm.nih.gov/pmc/articles/PMC4595739/

2. Hsiao, Y., (2017), SAGE Journal, Hammill Institute on Disabilities, Council for Learning Disabilities; https://journals.sagepub.com/doi/10.1177/1053451217712956

3. World Health Organization (2023), Preterm Birth https://www.who.int/news-room/fact-sheets/detail/preterm-birth

4. Bliss (2024), Statistics for babies admitted to neonatal units at full term, https://www.bliss.org.uk/research-campaigns/neonatal-care-statistics/statistics-for-babies-admitted-to-neonatal-units-at-full-term

5. Moving the Human Spirit (2023), Trauma-Informed Coaching, https://www.movingthehumanspirit.com/

6. Institute of Health Visiting (2022), Good Practice Points – Trauma-aware and trauma-informed practice: Working with families of children with a disability /difficulty, https://ihv.org.uk/wp-content/uploads/2022/08/GPP-Trauma-aware-and-trauma-informed-practice-FINAL-VERSION-8.8.22.pdf

7. Alderdice, F. (2022), National Institute for Health and Care Research, Neonatal care parents may need long-term support, https://evidence.nihr.ac.uk/alert/neonatal-care-parents-may-need-long-term-psychological-support/

8. Rubin, S., Malkinson, R., Witztum, E. (2020), National Institutes of Health, Traumatic Bereavements: Rebalancing the Relationship to the Decreased and the Death Story Using The Two-Track Model of Bereavement, https://www.ncbi.nlm.nih.gov/pmc/articles/PMC7523537/

9. World Health Organization, (2024) Newborn Mortality, https://www.who.int/news-room/fact-sheets/detail/newborn-mortality

10. Hsiao, Y., (2018), Parental Stress in Families of Children with Disabilities, SAGE Journal, https://journals.sagepub.com/doi/10.1177/1053451217712956

11. Lakhani, J., Mack, C., Kunyk, D., Manen, M., (2023), Sage Journals, Exploring and Supporting Parents' Stories of Loss in the NICU: A Narrative Study, https://journals.sagepub.com/doi/10.1177/10497323231201023

12. Anxiety Disorders, National Institute of Mental Health, (2024), https://www.nimh.nih.gov/health/topics/anxiety-disorders

13. Fincham, G., Strauss, C., Montero-Marin, J., Cavanagh, K., (2023), Effect of breathwork on stress and mental health: A meta-analysis of randomised-controlled trials, https://www.ncbi.nlm.nih.gov/pmc/articles/PMC9828383/

14. Beckers, T., Hermans, D., Lange,I., Luyten, L., Scheveneels, S., Vervliet, B., (2023), Nature Reviews Psychology, Understanding clinical fear and anxiety through the lens of human fear conditioning, https://www.ncbi.nlm.nih.gov/pmc/articles/PMC9933844/

15. DiFazio, D., (2013), Divorce and Children with Chronic Disorders: Diabetes as an Exemplar, Journal of Pediatric Nursing, Nursing Care of Children and Families, https://www.pediatricnursing.org/article/S0882-5963(13)00102-4/fulltext#:~:text=Parents%20of%20seriously%20or%20chronically%20ill%20children%20can,closeness%2C%20greater%20cohesion%20and%20increased%20support%20%28Lawrence%2C%202012

16. Flach, K., Gressler, N., Marcolino, M., Levandowski, D., (2022), Complicated Grief After the Loss of a Baby: A Systematic Review About Risk and Protective Factors for Bereaved Women, National Library of Medicine, https://www.ncbi.nlm.nih.gov/pmc/articles/PMC8747442/

17. Hansen, K., Davis, P., Hubbard, D., (2023), Trauma Informed Care in the Neonatal Intensive Care Unit, Journal of Social Work in End0of0Life and Palliative Care, https://www.tandfonline.com/doi/full/10.1080/15524256.2023.2262155

18. Hirsch, M., Classifications of Guilt, (1997), *Schuld und Schuldgefühl*. On the Psychoanalysis of Trauma and Introject, https://de.book-info.com/isbn/3-525-01435-X.htm

19. Paassen, F., (2021), On guilt and feelings of guilt: a psychodynamic perspective, Researchgate, https://www.researchgate.net/profile/Frans-Paassen?_tp=eyJjb250ZXh0Ijp7ImZpcnN0UGFnZSI6InB1YmxpY2F0aW9uIiwicGFnZSI6InB1YmxpY2F0aW9uIn19

ABOUT GIGI

Gigi Khonyongwa-Fernandez is a trauma-informed leadership coach, consultant, and advocate with a deeply personal connection to trauma and passion for resilience, healing, and finding joy. The mother of a surviving twin born four months prematurely and four angel babies, she integrates her lived experiences of trauma, healing, and hope into her work. She is an International Coach Federation (ICF) accredited Professional Coach and a Trauma-Informed Certified Coach (TICC), as well as the founder of GKF Coaching & Consulting and Families Blossoming LLC. Through these organizations, she supports neonatal/family-centered care and leadership and organizational wellness.

With an almost 20-year background in healthcare across two continents, Gigi combines her clinical and management expertise in this sector with compassionate and positive leadership. She specializes in trauma-informed coaching, maternal-infant health, and holistic leadership and organizational development, working with individuals, teams, and institutions across a wide range of various sectors. Some of her clients include the British Broadcasting Corporation (BBC), European Foundation for the Care of Newborn Infants (EFCNI), Fremantle Limited, March of Dimes, National Health Service, (NHS), NICU Parent Network (NPN), Prolacta

Bioscience, VML, William Grant & Sons, Ltd., PearnKandola, and the US Department of Treasury. An international speaker and advocate, she holds multiple global board appointments in the NICU and maternal-infant health spaces.

Gigi believes in and learns from the diverse beauty, flexibility, power, and dynamic nature of the human spirit and applies these lessons within her professional and personal life. Originally from the U.S., she now resides in London with her Spanish husband and British son, drawing inspiration from them, as well as her travels to over 25 countries and counting. From Rollercoasters to Carousels is her first book.

Feel free to connect with Gigi at: gigi@familiesblossoming.com

www.ingramcontent.com/pod-product-compliance
Lightning Source LLC
Chambersburg PA
CBHW051245020426
42333CB00025B/3059